RFID FOR LIBRARIES:
A Practical Approach

RFID FOR LIBRARIES:
A Practical Approach

NEERAJ KUMAR SINGH
Asstt. Librarian,
Panjab University, Chandigarh

Ess Ess Publications
New Delhi

RFID FOR LIBRARIES:
A Practical Approach

ISBN : 978-93-87698-19-2

First Published 2019

Published by:
Ess Ess Publications
4831/24, Ansari Road,
Darya Ganj,
New Delhi-110 002.
INDIA
Phones: 23260807, 41563444
Fax: 41563334
E-mail: info@essessreference.com
www.essessreference.com

Cover Design by *Patch Creative Unit*

Printed and bound in India

Dedicated to
My father
Late Shri Shambhu Prasad Singh

Contents

Contents

Central University of Punjab
(Established vide an Act No. 25(2009) of Parliament)

Prof. R. K. Kohli
FNA, FASc, FNASc, FNAAS
Certified Sr. Ecologist, ESA,USA
JC Bose National Fellow
Vice-Chancellor

Ref. No.: CUPB/1786

Dated : 26-10-18

Foreword

This monograph entitled "**Implementation of RFID in libraries: a practical approach**" is a rich blend of rigorous systematic research and practical experiences of an energetic professional. It provides several new insights into the field of RFID (radio frequency identification) applications in libraries - focal points of accumulated knowledge. Every library is expected to provide maximum opportunities to its users and ensure optimum utilisation of its available resources. Hence, consistent efforts for seeking useful technological aids to improve their services is required. Due to the low cost of the barcode technology, most of the libraries around the world are using it for circulation management. However, there are many constraints related to it. At the same time, it is becoming very difficult for the libraries to satisfy the increasing demands of the users worldwide and manage their vast resources in an optimal way. Thus comes the need to implement newer technologies to ensure the security of library collections, and improve resource circulation and inventory management.

RFID technology has been in use in many fields for quiet sometime. However, though affordable, its application in libraries in India is still at a nascent stage. It is, therefore, high time to study the adoption process of this useful technology in libraries and evaluate problems and benefits, apart from formulating the best procedures for the same. The adoption of this technology by libraries promises a solution that would make it possible to inventory hundreds of thousands of items in their collection in days instead of months. Fortunately, librarians known as early adopters of technology have started using it.

This book, an outcome of extensive research work done by the author for doctorate degree contains many interesting findings that are worth applying in practice in every library. It also presents several new and intriguing questions, and pathways for further research. In my opinion, it can be of use to every academic institutions and centers of research. The practicing library and information professionals, students who aspire to be future librarians as well as the administrators of institutions who have to provide funds for libraries will benefit immensely from the contents of this book. I am aware, the author has himself gained rich experience during the implementation of RFID based system in his library. His such experiences can be highly beneficial for the library and information community. This important title will facilitate the understanding of RFID technology from a library perspective. The useful suggestions/insights given in this book will surely be beneficial in terms of better utilisation of available resources and improvement of libraries.

I congratulate the author for producing such a useful book and sincerely wish him to keep contributing for posterity through creation of new knowledge.

(R K Kohli)
Vice- Chancellor
26-October 2018

City Campus, Mansa Road, Bathinda-151 001, (Punjab) India
Tel. +91-164-243 0586; Fax. +91-164-286 4111; rkkohli45@yahoo.com, vc@cup.ac.in, www.cup.ac.in, www.rkkohli.com

Preface

For a common man most of the modern technologies seem to work magically, especially as their operations are not readily visible and they operate automatically. A relatively new technology called Radio Frequency Identification (RFID), gives exactly this kind of a feeling. Librarians worldwide are early adapters of new technologies and have been following closely the advancements in the field of RFID technology. RFID technology is a big leap forward over using bar codes on library materials. RFID tags have revolutionized and radically redesigned the process of handling library materials. But this option is expensive. The handicap in adopting the RFID technology in libraries is that the technology is not fully developed and the tags are susceptible to wear and tear. The return on investment (ROI) is also unclear. While most of the libraries now have information technology expertise within their organizations, RFID technology know how is not familiar to them. The title of this book "RFID for Libraries: A practical approach" is self explanatory in that it examines what RFID technology is and how it works in the library scenario. The book reviews the development of RFID technology and its effects on library operations over the last couple of decades. An assessment of current implementation of the technology in libraries and the lessons learnt provide suggestions to overcome the issues faced at practical level in any library. The concluding chapter looks at the future technologies developing and how they might be applied in libraries.

The author was actively involved throughout the recent implementation of RFID based system for his library and has gained rich experience in the process. The libraries planning to implement this technology can benefit from the rich practical knowledge of the author given in this book. The latest technologies contribute greatly in the functioning and improvement of library services. Presented from a library perspective this title will assist the library and information community in understanding RFID technology.

Acknowledgements

Many people contributed to this book in innumerable ways, and I am grateful to all of them.

First of all, I would like to give my sincere thanks to my supervisor, Prof. Preeti Mahajan, Department of Library and Information Scince, Panjab University, Chandigarh. Her guidance, wisdom, unending encouragement and constructive suggestions, insatiable hunger for quality work has ever kept me on my toes and inspired me to produce something up to her expectations. Her role will remain a source of enduring inspiration to me throughout my life.

I would like to express my thanks to Ms. Navjeet Kaur, Deputy librarian, A C Joshi Library, Panjab University, Chandigarh for her encouragement and support..

I would like to thank all the librarians and library staff as well as the users of nine institutions selected under the study.

1

Understanding RFID Technology

RFID, the acronym for Radio Frequency Identification, is a technology that uses radio frequency wave transmission for identifying a person or object. There are many technologies in the market, such as bar code, magnetic ink, voice recognition, optical character recognition, touch memory, smart card, biometrics, etc. An Automatic Identification (AutoID) technology that makes use of radio waves for communication within a system of integrated circuits with the help of its components i.e. tags, readers, software and middleware to identify items is the RFID technology. RFID refers to a technology system in which a tag communicates a radio frequency signal that is interpreted by a reader.[1] The radio waves that are transmitted by an antenna interact with an integrated circuit embedded on an RFID tag, that in turn sends back these waves to a reader. The reader then converts those waves into digital information that instantly identifies the item that responds.[2]

RFID has become one of the most important applications in businesses and establishments today. One of the world's largest retailer Wal- Mart and the United States Department of Defense has used the RFID technology widely which has made the benefits of using RFID widely known to other groups of people, businesses and companies. Many other large companies have also realized the benefits of RFID for production and distribution of goods and services. The advantages range from accurate and fast inventory management to theft detection. RFID has been applied in many diverse areas such as logistics, supply chain management, medical services, warehouse management, libraries, highway tolling, access control building, homeland security applications, aviation security, tracking luggage at airports, Automated Vehicle Identification (AVI) systems, etc.

The world's largest passenger airplane, the new Airbus A380, uses more than 10,000 RFID tags on the removable pieces and also on those items that need periodic maintenance or replacement. In healthcare services the hospitals are applying the capability of RFID tags to protect patient information from medical errors and to protect babies from abduction. Similarly to prevent the abuse of regulated substances and counterfeiting the pharmaceutical companies are using RFID tags on drug containers.[3] This helps them to track the movement of their consignments. Libraries tag items by using the RFID technology so that to the misplaced books can be quickly located on the library shelves and also to enable the function of self checkouts and check-ins of library items. The problem of higher cost of this technology will be tackled by competition generated as more manufacturers of RFID equipment and software solutions are entering the market. Due to this growing competition it is expected that the price of this technology will continue to fall and as a result its practical applications will continue to grow.[4] This market development will lead eventually to more libraries adopting the use of the technology as many were hesitating to use it due to scarcity of funds.

1.1. DEFINITIONS OF RFID

- According to Brown[5], "RFID is an automatic identification technology that put "tags" on objects (documents, people, animals, vehicles, containers, etc.) so they can be identified, tracked and managed automatically utilizing radio frequency equipment and supporting computer systems".
- According to MacMillan Dictionary (online)[6], "RFID is a technology that uses labels that produce radio signals to identify things such as goods, farm animals and vehicle. RFID has replaced bar codes in some shops."
- According to Automatic Identification and Data Capture (AIDC)[7], "Radio Frequency identification is a technology that uses radio waves to transfer data between a rcadcr and an electronic tag which is attached to a particular object. Typical uses are for object identification and tracking."

1.2. HISTORY OF RFID TECHNOLOGY

RFID technology is not a new invention, though in the recent years it is getting more and more attention. To trace the history of RFID technology is a difficult task. As early as in the year 1886, a German physicist Heinrich Hertz discovered that solid objects reflected radio waves from their surface. Radar was discovered in the year 1935. The word 'Radar' is an acronym that stands for Radio Detection and Ranging and was discovered by a Scottish physicist Sir Robert Alexander Watson-Watt. Radar was used to warn the host country of approaching planes even while they were flying miles away from it. This system was being used by the Britishers, Germans, Japanese and Americans. Watt led the development of a practical version of this device, which entered service in 1938 under the code name Chain Home. There is a general consensus that RFID evolved from the technology invented during the World War II so that enemy aircrafts could be identified, known as 'Identification: Friend or Foe' (IFF) systems.[8]

The problem with the Radar technology was that that it wasn't possible to identify the enemy planes from the host country's own planes that were coming back from a mission. Another British expert scientist Watson Watt was head of a project to secretly develop the first active Identify Friend or Foe (IFF) system. Under this project a transmitter was fixed on the British planes that began broadcasting a signal as soon as it received signals from the ground radar stations that would identify the plane as friend. The radar crew on the ground was thus alerted by this crude method as to whether the planes approaching were their own planes or those of the allies. This was essentially the first passive RFID system. These two technologies, Radar and IFF, conceptually formed the beginning of what we know today as RFID. RFID technology works on the same basic concepts i.e. when a signal is received by a transponder it activates and in the case of a passive system reflects back a signal or in case of an active system broadcasts a signal.

Mario W. Cardullo lays claim to have received the first U.S. patent for inventing an active RFID tag that had a rewritable memory on 23 January, 1973. In the same year, a Californian entrepreneur, Charles Walton, patented a passive transponder that could be used to unlock a door without the using a key. In keyless access there is a card with that has an embedded transponder that transmits a signal to a reader located near the door. This reader unlocks the door on detecting a valid unique identity number stored on the RFID tag. The following table provides a glimpse of the timeline of the major RFID milestones reached over the past 60 years.[9]

Table 1.1. Time line of RFID[10,11,12]

Decade	Event
1940s	As a result of the World War II a major development effort was made and Radar was refined and adopted.
1950s	Marked by early laboratory experiments of RFID technology and explorations.
1960s	Theory of RFID developed and field trials of its application started.
1970s	Explosion of RFID development and its application for electronic article surveillance (EAS) to counter theft cases; to improve animal and vehicle tracking, and use for factory automation. Tests of RFID accelerate.
1980s	Commercial and industrial applications of RFID enter the mainstream market.
1990s	Saw the emergence of standards of RFID technology. RFID system deployed, at electronic toll collection plazas, throughout the United States. RFID started becoming a part of common man's life with a single tag having the capability of handling multiple applications such as EAS, fare collection, access to car park, gated community, campus etc.
2000s	Development and expansion in applications of RFID in supply chain management, healthcare/ pharmaceuticals and library systems. Major retailers mandated that their suppliers implement case level tagging by January 2005 which sparked rapid RFID research and development.
2010 to Present	RFID continues to grow with the adoption of EPC codes (Electronic Product Codes). The present situation is that RFID technology is being used all over the world in hundreds of different applications in diverse fields.

1.2.1. Pre 1940s

By the the 19th century, Faraday, Maxwell, Hertz and others developed a complete set of laws describing the nature and state of the technology. Many scientists including Marconi, Alexanderson, Baird, Watson and others applied the laws of other technologies to the radio communications technology as well as in radar technology in the beginning of the year 1896. The work done by these scientists laid the foundation on which many later technologies including RFID developed. World War II triggered much advancement in radio frequency communications and the radar technology was evolved. In the years following the war, scientists and engineers continued their research work and sought areas of use for this technology increasingly in the civilian sectors. A research paper by Harry Stockman, strongly influencing later developments, entitled "Communications by means of Reflected Power" published in 1948 was considered as the root of RFID technology.[13]

1.2.2. 1950s— Exploring the technology

In the following decade i.e. 1950s, the RFID technology had started to fascinate scientists thus many technologies similar to RFID were explored in detail by researchers. Many landmark papers were published, notable among them were F.L. Vernon's "Applications of the Microwave Homodyne" and D.B. Harris's "Radio Transmission Systems with Modulatable Passive Responders." During this decade the U.S. military services started using an early form of RFID technology in their aircrafts called Identification, Friend or Foe (IFF).[14]

1.2.3. 1960s—Early field trials

The 1960s were an introduction to RFID. However, its expansion came on the horizon later in the 1970s. R.F. Harrington did research in the electromagnetic field theory as applied to RFID that was reported in "Field Measurements Using Active Scatterers" and "Theory of Loaded Scatterers". Many RFID inventors started to emerge who made inventions in the field such as Robert Richardson's "Remotely Activated Radio Frequency Powered Devices"; Otto Rittenback's "Communication by Radar Beams"; J.H. Vogelman's "Passive Data Transmission Techniques Utilizing Radar Beams," and J.P.

Vinding's "Interrogator- Responder Identification System." By the end of 1960s some commercial applications of RFID also started. With a view to develop the security aspect in the RFID applications Electronic Article Surveillance (EAS) equipment for anti-theft and such applications as Sensormatic and Checkpoint were developed. The examples of these are the security gates placed at the entrance of department stores, establishments, residences etc. to check theft. They were simple, 1-bit systems with the limited function of detection of the presence of RFID tags on items rather than being used for identifying them. In the years to come EAS became the first widely used commercial application of RFID technology.14

1.2.4. 1970s—Early-adopter applications

The decade of 1970s witnessed an exponential growth of the RFID technology. Increasingly the academic institutions, businesses, large corporations and even the governments became interested in RFID applications. Advances in the field of RFID were notably made through research. Los Alamos Scientific Laboratory in 1975 made public a great deal of its RFID research. A paper was written by Alfred Koelle, Steven Depp and Robert Freyman was published that was entitled "Short-Range Radio-telemetry for Electronic Identification Using Modulated Backscatter". Many large contemporary companies such as Raytheon, RCA and Fairchild started the work focused on development of electronic identification system technology. As a result of their efforts by the year 1978, a microwave transponder that was passive in nature had been invented. At the same time several agencies of the government became interested in the technology. The Port Authority of New York and New Jersey continued their experiments in the field of transportation applications that were developed by GE, Westinghouse, Philips and Glenayre, although the technology was not adopted officially by them. In the United States the U.S. Federal

Highway Administration organised a conference to explore the application of electronic identification technology in the areas of vehicle and transportation sytems. In the late 1970s a number of small companies began to emerge that focused on RFID technology. As the decade of 1970s drew to an end, most of the research being carried out in RF electronics and electromagnetic with reference to RFID was complete. As a consequence the research in computers and in the field of information technology, networks and interrogators had started. This was critical for the development of RFID systems and its applications. This led to the birth of the PC and the ARPANET which became a predecessor to the Internet.[15]

1.2.5. 1980s—Commercialization

The 1980s saw the popularization and wider commercial uses of the RFID technology. The systems at that time were simple. Examples of the application of the technology include management of livestock, personnel access systems and keyless entry. Applications in the transportation sector emerged late in the decade. The Association of American Railroads and the Container Handling Cooperative Program played an active part in taking RFID initiatives and aimed at developing RFID-enabled railroad cars. The world's first toll application of RFID was in Norway in 1987, followed by Dallas in 1989. The Port Authority of New York and New Jersey also started using the RFID technology in a commercial project for the buses that passed through the Lincoln Tunnel. All the RFID systems used during this decade were proprietary systems as yet no standards of RFID were available. There was no interoperability between systems and there was little competition in the RFID industry which led to high costs for implementing the technology. This was the major impediment in the growth of the industry.[16]

1.2.6. 1990s—RFID enters the mainstream

The 1990s were a significant landmark in the

development journey of RFID as it had finally begun to percolate the mainstream market of business and technology. During the decade, RFID toll plazas had been installed and that could operate at high speeds, enabling the vehicles to pass through toll gates uninterrupted and without having to stop at toll plazas or barriers. Thus tolls could be regulated with the aid of video cameras only without deploying any manpower. Thus RFID toll systems were deployed widely across the United States. Local toll agencies started integrating their RFID systems so as to have the added advantage of paying of multiple tolls by the drivers through the same account. This took the technology one step further. Texas Instruments began its system called TIRIS. New RFID applications were developed in this system such as Exxon-Mobil's Speed pass for dispensing fuel, as well as for vehicle access. In fact, many large companies in the United States and Europe started taking interest in developing RFID during 1990s which included such companies as Philips, Mikron, Alcatel, Bosch, etc.[17]

The widespread use of PC's and Internet by the early 1990s increased and this is an evidence of the fact that information technology research was well developed in this period. Now in order to develop commercial viability of the systems the RFID industry had to overcome the problem of expensive tags. Materials technology during the 1990s, made advances in with most of the research related to the working of semiconductors. Chip making big companies such as IBM, Intel, Motorola and AMD, brought out in the market cost- effective tags. This development resulted in investment capital flow to RFID research and thus many projects got fillip. By the end of the decade large-scale tests on "smart label" had begun.

The RFID system in the market was proprietary system until the 1990s. This was recognized as a barrier to growth of the industry and thus the efforts to standardize the technology began. Several organizations including the European Conference of Postal and Telecommunications Administrations (CEPT) and the International Organization of Standards (ISO) got working on formulating guidelines and standards. As a result in 1999 the Auto-ID Center was established at M.I.T. These organizations worked on bringing out standards for RFID technology applications and its implementation particularly with reference to supply chain management and asset management. Although the inclination towards bringing out standards started in the late 1990s, yet the two projects successfully completed were:

- The ISO 18000 series of standards: These standards specified how information between readers and tags should be communicated in an RFID system.
- The Auto-ID Centre's standards: They specified standards on all aspects of an RFID asset tracking system operation. They were subsequently passed onto EAN.[18]

1.2.7. 2000s—RFID deployment

By the beginning of the 21st century, it became obvious that RFID technology would someday replace the bar code systems. A lot of interest of the industry was focused on the implications RFID technology in the areas of distribution of products, the retail industry and the cost involved. In the year 2003 RFID got a fillip in particular as Michelin, the largest tire manufacturing company, had begun testing of the possibility of an RFID transponder embedded in its fleet of tires that would enable them to be tracked electronically. Many other retailers and manufacturers in the sector followed suit, such as Proctor & Gamble, Target and Gillette.

In the year 2003 many developments took place, the Auto-ID Centre merged into EPC Global and the technology developed by EPC was adopted by giant industries like Wal-Mart and Department of Defence as well as the RFID industry. They wanted their suppliers to begin employing RFID technology by 2005. The combined huge size of the operations of these companies constituted an enormous market for RFID. The standards that were developed by EPC were adopted in 2006 by ISO also which gave the RFID industry a single point guidance. As a result of the convergence of all standards many benefits were derived by the RFID industry. It led to competitive market in the industry that in turn lowered the cost of RFID components and hastened the adoption of RFID technology by many ventures. Soon new areas of application for RFID in a number of varied industries emerged. In the near future, RFID technology is expected to grow exponentially and be firmly a part of the mainstream market and will become an integral component of our everyday lives, just like television, PCs and mobile phones.[19]

1.3. COMPONENTS OF RFID SYSTEM

The components of RFID system are the following:

1. Tag
2. Antenna
3. Reader
4. Middleware
5. Server

The following figure indicates the overview of the RFID system:

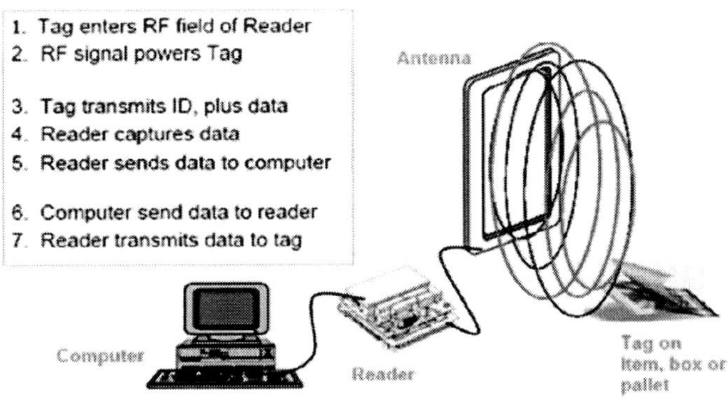

Fig. 1.1 Overview of an RFID system[24]

1.3.1. RFID tag

The Tag is a very small radio transmitter or responder that has a certain amount of internal memory called the Electrically Erasable Programmable Read-Only Memory (EEPROM). In this memory the tag stores information about the item. This information may be as brief as only the unique ID number, or sometimes much more detailed such as include the manufacturing date and composition of the item, its location etc. The tags that contain the relevant information are called the programmed tags. When such programmed tags pass near a reader i.e. through a field generated by a it they transmit the information stored on them back to the reader, by which the item is identified.[20] The passive RFID tag draws power from the field created by the reader to function and uses it to power the microchip's circuit.[21] This powered chip then generates the radio waves that the tag reflects back to the reader, which modulates the new waves into digital data form and then transmits it to the host computer.[22] This communication process between the reader and tag is governed by one of several protocols in the field, such as the ISO 15693 and ISO 18000-3 for HF or the ISO 18000-6 and EPC for UHF.[23]

An RFID tag is a tiny device that can also be called a radio barcode, smart label, transponder, or smart tag. The main components of the RFID tag are two i.e. a small silicon chip with an integrated circuit that stores a unique identification number and second is an antenna that sends and receives radio waves.

The antenna consists of a metallic conductive coil that is flat and a chip that is very small in size almost less than half a millimeter[25]. These two components i.e. the chip and the antenna are attached to a flat sheet of plastic that can be fixed physically on an item. The tags are normally quite small and thin so that they can be easily embedded within posters, tickets, packaging, plastic cards, clothing labels, books etc. These tags can be read from a distance so as the identity, position, or state of the object they are embedded in can be known remotely. The tags are the heart of the RFID system as the information that describes the object being tracked by RFID readers via the radio waves is embedded on them. In order to obtain the information stored on a tag, a reader emits a signal towards the RFID tag that causes the tag to transmit the information back to the reader. The reader then translates the signal to a digital format before transmitting it to a management system.[26] The Fig. 1.2 below shows the structure of a tag:

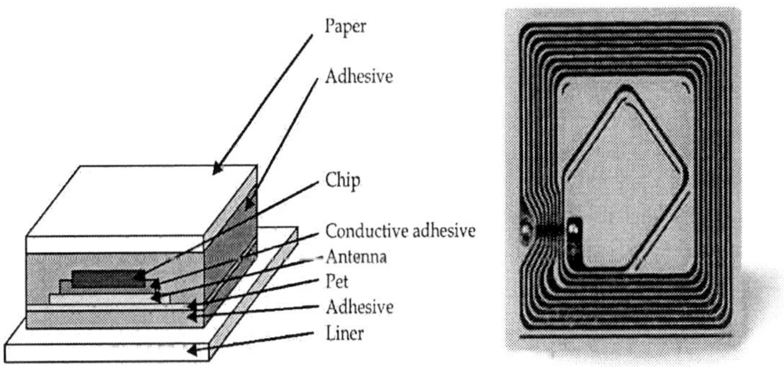

Fig. 1.2. Tag construction[27]

The tags can be classified into various categories depending upon the source of power, frequency, functionality and protocols.

1.3.1.1. According to the **source of the power**, the tags can be: active, passive, semi-active or sensor.

(a) Active tag : Tags having an active radio frequency (RF) transmitter are called Active Tags. They use batteries that power the chip so that it can communicate with the reader. Such Tags have a read distance of 300 feet (100 meters) i.e. they can respond from a distance of 300 feet or more but they are quiet expensive. They are used in automatic toll-road payment systems and can be read even when the vehicle they are embedded in is moving at a speed of up to 100 miles an hour and the readers have the capability of reading up to a thousand tags per second. Active tags can be used for regulating temperature and report any temperature fluctuations of refrigerated products while they are in transit, and convey if that is unacceptable. This function is possible only if the tags are equipped with built-in sensors. They are also more secure. They have comparatively a larger memory than that of the passive tags and are capable of processing more information. They can thus be used in multifarious applications at various levels like container or even box level tracking, people tracking, long-range monitoring, real-time location, area security, sensor monitoring etc.

(b) Passive tag : The passive tags do not have any battery embedded on them and they function by drawing power from a reader. The Reader sends radio waves that produce a current in the antenna of a tag which in turn is used to power the circuit of a microchip. This activated chip then transmits the waves that are sent back by the tag to the reader. Passive tags have a lesser read range of approximately 30 feet. They cannot function individually and require the presence of a reader. The read range of passive tags is limited i.e. approx. four or five meters in UHF. The passive tags have a much longer lifecycle as they do not their own power source. They are also cheaper to produce because of their on-board circuitry is minimal. Consequently the Passive tags are flat, in label form. Though they have shorter read range than the active tags, they cost less and offer a virtually unlimited operational lifetime. The passive tags have been found to be more suitable applications for tagging individual items such as for supermarket checkouts and smart cards. They are also most suitable for tagging library items.

(c) Semi-active tag : These tags have an embedded battery but contain no radio transmitter. The integrated circuit (IC) of the tag is powered by the battery which helps it to convert the reflected signal. Because the tag does not have a radio transmitter a reflected signal is required for it to work. The advantage of this type of tags is that they need not to be powered by the reader. As a result low-power readers can be used and more data can be stored on the semi-active tags. This type of tag can best work when coupled with environmental sensors used for temperature reading, pressure reading and control, relative humidity reporting, Global Positioning System (GPS), etc. and can be used to get longer read range (up to 50 m). The sensors of the tag require continuous power, thus these tags have embedded battery. Due to battery these tags are larger in size and are heavy, have higher cost, and limited life.

(d) Sensor tag : It incorporates a sensor as well as has memory on the tag. Sensor RFID Tags are best used in applications used to detect environmental changes and events. They communicate this received data to an RFID reader. These are used in telemetry products and ideally work best in situations where measurements need to be taken in real time and have to be captured remotely and automatically. Depending on the type of sensor embedded on the tags they can be used to sense changes in motion, humidity, temperature, pressure, etc. RFID sensor tags are becoming widely popular for use in such applications as measuring air pressure in vehicle tires or temperatures in cold food supply chain and drug use monitoring.

1.3.1.2. According to the **frequency**, the tags can be classified as:

(a) Low Frequency (LF) - 125 - 135 KHz;

(b) High Frequency (HF) -13.56 MHz;

(c) Ultra High Frequency (UHF) - 860-960 MHz;

(d) Microwave Frequency - 2.45 and 5.8 GHz.

1.3.1.3. According to the **functions** they perform, the RFID tags are classified into different classes by the Auto-ID Center and later by EPC Global. According to the basic structure and function tags can be classified into five classes in as follows:

Table 1.2. RFID Class Structure[26]

	Class	Functionality
1	Identity Tags	Purely passive, identification only
2	Higher	Purely passive, identification + Functionality Tags other functions e.g. read/write memory
3	Semi-Passive Tags	Not purely passive as battery power embedded on them
4	Active 'ad hoc' Tags	Able to Communicate with other active tags
5	Reader Tags	Able to both provide power for and communicate with other tags, i.e. they can act as a reader and transmit and receive radio waves

1.3.2. Readers and Antenna

An RFID system consists of another basic component the Reader also called the Interrogator. The reader units are technically transceivers i.e. they are a combination of a transmitter and a receiver. The general role of the Reader is both to send a query to the tag and also receive data from it. The basic function of a RFID reader is to receive signal from the RFID tags and convert these radio waves into a form that can be passed on to the middleware software. The RFID reader communicates with the RFID chip by using antennas. The Reader can perform the functions of both reading the information stored on the RFID tags and also update them with any new information that needs to be updated. Hence, two tasks are accomplished by the RFID reader: firstly it receives commands sent by the application software and secondly it communicates with the RFID tags. RFID Readers may have an integrated antenna or a separate one. The RFID reader station can either be a fixed unit or a handheld one. The handheld Readers have both the reader and antenna. In the larger systems the antennas are usually separate from the reader. RFID reader antennas are available in variety of sizes and shapes. In material handling systems they can be embedded into desktops and other furniture, mounted into EAS gates, or integrated into the conveyer or other components.

The workstation that carries the application software, the reader and the antenna are all clubbed together as parts of one device, in the case of handheld readers. However, at a later stage, the data that has been exchanged with the tags may be stored in a main processing unit that depends upon the type of application used. An RFID reader is practically a connection between the application software and the antenna that transmits radio waves towards the tags. The radio waves generated by the antenna travel in the surrounding space and in this way the data is wirelessly transmitted towards the tags that are in the range of the antenna. The Readers operate at different RF frequencies and even within the same frequency, different communication protocols may be used by them. How tags and readers communicate is governed by rules that are called the Air interface protocols. Reader Talks First (RTF) or Tag Talks First (TTF) are the two common families of protocols. In RTF protocol, the tag waits for a command or a signal by the reader before communicating the data. Whereas in TTF protocol, the tag, while it is in the RF field, is powered up and sends information on a continuous basis without waiting for a specific command from the reader.[28]

According to Ward (2006),[26] the following are the two main types of RFID Readers:

(i) Read-only: they function with purely passive Class 1 tags

(ii) Read/Write : those have the capability to write new information on a tag that is equipped with a read/write memory.

1.3.3. Middleware

In an RFID system applications of both a middleware and software are required. The function of the Middleware is to manage the flow of data between the reader and the backend application. The principle purpose of middleware is to extract data from the RFID tags; however, in addition to this it manages flow of data to the station at the backend. In addition the middleware performs various other functions such as basic data filtering, integration of the reader etc. RFID middleware helps in multiple ways from retrieving data from readers, generate inventory movement notifications, filter data fed to the application software, monitor the tag and reader network function, capture the history, to the ultimate analysis of tag-read events for application and optimization.

1.3.4. Server

An RFID system configured server is a gateway that communicates among the various components. Once the server receives the information from the reader it checks it against its database stored on it and exchanges this information with the circulation database of the integrated Library Management System. Typically the server contains a transaction database so that reports can be generated.[29]

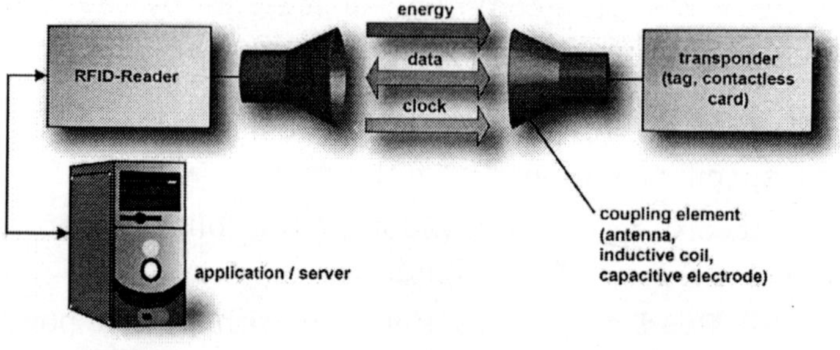

Fig. 1.3. Main components of the RFID system[30]

1.4. RFID FREQUENCY

The radio waves are the medium for communication between the components of an RFID system and the size of these radio waves is referred to as its Frequency. This frequency enables the reader to communicate wirelessly with the tags. For the deployment of an RFID system several frequency bands are available in which RFID systems can operate i.e. the Low Frequency (LF), High Frequency (HF), Ultrahigh Frequency (UHF) and Microwave Frequency bands. The choice of selecting the operating frequency depends upon the requirement of the application it has to be put to, such as the reading distance required, non-interference with other applications using radio systems in the vicinity, data communication speed desired and the size of the antenna. Whereas, low frequency systems can function by using passive tags, the higher frequency systems can operate only with the active tags. Generally, if the frequency is low it will provide a short read range and also a slow data read rate, whereas it means an increased capability for near reading or reading on metal or liquid surfaces. Due to the limitation of power at lower frequencies, passive tags are not able to transmit their data further than a few feet. At higher frequencies, the reading distance between the active tags with internal batteries and the reader is generally higher. The characteristic that is influenced by the frequency is not only the reading distance but other parameters such as the electrical interference with other existing systems that is higher for frequencies lower than 300 KHz and decreases as the frequency increases. The rate of data communication between the tags and the reader from Kbit/s to Mbit/s for frequencies lower than 300KHz is greater than those with a frequency of 300MHz.31 Different frequencies have distinct properties and features. The selection of frequency to be used for a given application depends on the demands of the area and the best match of these requirements to the frequency properties has to be sought. There are four key RFID frequency bands used today:

1.4.1. Low-Frequency (LF) 125-134 KHz

The low-frequency RFID systems typically have the frequency of 125 KHz, though some systems may operate higher frequency of 134 KHz as well. This band of frequency is characterised by a shorter read range that is less than 0.5m or 1.5 ft. They are marked by a slower read speed in comparison to any of the other higher frequencies. The LF RFID systems are the best option to be fixed on items that have high water or metal content as they can be read accurately. As compared to higher frequency options the LF systems are less sensitive to interference. Applications of low-frequency RFID systems are typically in areas of animal tracking, access control, healthcare services, product authentication, etc. There are differences in the frequency and power levels used in the LF spectrum worldwide thus it is not a standard application.

1.4.2. High-Frequency (HF) 13.56 MHz

High-frequency RFID systems function at 13.56 MHz. As they operate at a higher frequency they are characterized by a higher read speed and greater range than the LF systems. These tags have the lowest cost of all RFID tags. The read range of these frequency tags is typically that of less than 1 meter or 3 feet. They have better ability to read tags on items with high water or metal content than that of the UHF systems though not as good as the LF systems. HF systems mostly have applications in such areas as smart cards and smart shelves as they have a good ability for tracking goods at the item level. They are also at present used in tracking healthcare services, patients, library books, product authentication and airline baggage. Data log maintenance for delicate equipment that needs to be checked regularly like the fire safety systems is another common application area of these tags. There are various standards regarding the HF systems, prominent being the ISO 15693 standard that is being used for governing the tracking of items.

1.4.3. Ultrahigh Frequency (UHF) 860-960 MHz

In Ultrahigh frequency RFID the bandwidth of 860 to 930MHz is utilized. A UHF tag typically has a price range more or less the same as that of the HF tags. They have high read range of up to 3m or 9.5 ft. and have much faster data transfer rate than the systems using HF, though this rate is still slower than the Microwave based RFID systems. The main short coming of the UHF systems is that they have a limited ability to read tags on items that are either surrounded or contain high water or metal content. This is the typical frequency recommended for distribution chain management and in logistics. It is also the basis for the Auto- ID Center's standards for Electronic Product Code (EPC). Another primary application of this frequency is in the supply chain management and as it has a greater read range over the other ranges. This greater read range provided by the UHF frequency is also the rationale for its wide use on highways for electronic toll system, manufacturing applications and for parking access.[32]

1.4.4. Microwave 2.45 GHZ

Microwave frequency RFID systems operate at a frequency of 2.45GHz or 5.8GHz. The microwave RFID systems are the most expensive although they are marked by having a limited read range of up to 1m or 3 ft. However, they offer the highest data read rates. In addition, it is unsuitable for many applications as the microwave based systems are not suitable for items with high water or metal content. Currently, microwave frequency is restricted to specialized applications only such as in tracking airline baggage or for electronic toll collection.[33]

1.5. RFID STANDARDS AND REGULATIONS

A very important aspect of any technology to flourish is having standards and regulations associated with it.

RFID standards have been created to ensure that products are inter-operable. These provide guidelines to companies to develop complementary and interoperable tags, readers, software, etc. In RFID, standards can be applied to various facets such as to the format of tags; the content of the coded information stored on the tags; the frequencies and protocols that are used by the tags and readers to communicate their data etc. Various standards have been formulated globally that cover four key areas of RFID system applications: (i) Air Interface Standards used for basic data communication between the tag and the reader; (ii) Data Content and Encoding i.e. numbering schemes; (iii) Conformance for testing of RFID systems; and (iv) Interoperability between applications and RFID systems.[33] The ISO Standards define the Air Interface communication between reader-to-tag and tag-to-reader and govern the Communication protocol, types of Signal Modulation, Data coding and frames, rates of Data Transmission and Anti-collision etc. Mainly the reader power emissions and allocation of frequency bands are controlled by Regulations.[34]

The main problem related to RFID standards is that most RFID applications have been closed systems as there are no universally established standards. There are several industry specific bodies at the international, national and regional level that are involved in the development of RFID standards, including the International Organisation for Standardisation (ISO), EPC global, International Electro-technical Commission (IEC), International Tele-communications Union (ITU), Federal Communications Commission (FCC), European Conference of Postal and Telecommunications Administrations (CEPT), European Telecommunications Standards Institutes (ETSI), British Standards Institute (BSI), American National Standards Institute (ANSI), etc. However, the two main organizations globally involved in drafting standards for governing the RFID technology are the International Organization for

Standardization (ISO) and EPC global.[35]

1.5.1. The International Organization for Standardization (ISO)

The main contributor to the standardization of RFID is the International Organization for Standardization (ISO). The ISO works in collaboration with the International Electrotechnical Commission (IEC) on some aspects. ISO has developed standards for all areas of RFID including automatic identification and item management. This organization has evolved international standards for various areas of RFID application, principally in animal identification called the ISO 11784 and 11785 that was further refined by ISO 14223/1 and in the area of contactless smart cards called the ISO 10536, ISO 14443 and ISO 15693. Various standards in other areas that have a specific application focus have also been developed that include freight container identification using 2.45GHz transponders (ISO 10374) and data carriers for tools and clamping devices (ISO 69873). The standards developed by ISO, known as the ISO 18000 series, cover the air interface protocol for systems that are used to track goods in the supply chain. They cover the major frequencies used in RFID systems around the world. The seven parts are:[27 36]

- ISO/IEC 18000-1 Part 1 – Reference architecture and definition of parameters
- ISO/IEC 18000-2 Part 2 - Parameters for Air Interface Communications below 135 kHz
- ISO/IEC 18000-3 Part 3 - Parameters for Air Interface Communications at 13.56 MHz
- ISO/IEC 18000-4 Part 4 - Parameters for Air Interface Communications at 2.45 GHz
- ISO/IEC 18000-5 Part 5 - Parameters for Air Interface Communications at 5.8 GHz –(abandoned project).

- ISO/IEC 18000-6 Part 6 - Parameters for Air Interface Communications at 860 to 930MHz
- ISO/IEC 18000-7 Part 7 - Parameters for Air Interface Communications at 433 MHz

1.5.2. EPC Standards

EPC Global started the mission of formulating Standards so that every object is assigned a unique Electronic Product Code (EPC) by which it can be identified. They planned to implement a global network so that every item in the supply chain can be tracked throughout its journey. They invested large resources for research and development in creating the required infrastructure and to specificy and standardize the EPC tags. EPC Global focused their efforts primarily on UHF systems.

To promote the maximum usage of RFID technology in the information rich and fast-moving trading networks, EPC Global is the leader in developing the industry- driven standards for the Electronic Product Code™ (EPC). The Auto-ID Center has envisioned a next generation Electronic Product Code standard that will be used for identifying items and services. Their intention is not to replace the existing bar code standards but to formulate a system for companies to migrate from the established bar code standards to the newly formulated EPC standards. Similar to the Global Trade Item Number (GTIN) on GS1 barcodes, the EPC is a unique number that is the key that contains information that has been used for identification of specific items in the supply chain within the EPC global network.34 However, EPC is a step further in that whereas GTIN can only distinguish the category of products such as a corn can from a chocolate box, EPC can identify a product by its specific brand also by using its unique ID information. Huge amount of dynamic data can be associated with the EPC number and that data can be made available by providing access to additional information stored in databases. The encoded EPC number is embedded on the microchip of RFID tags.[37] This EPC number can be from the tag can be linked with the detailed data held in a secured database, to retrieve such information as an item origination; its manufacturing date etc. The EPC is the key that can unlock the information contained within the EPC global Network just as the GTIN on the barcode or vehicle identification number (VIN) can. As such an EPC tag is secure as it does not carry any identifiable personal information.[38]

Previously only Class 0 and Class 1 tags were manufactured by EPC global. The Class 0 tags are read-only tags that are programmed at the time the microchip is manufactured whereas Class 1 tag is a simple, passive, read-only tag with the ability to be programmed one-time in the field with non-volatile memory. Shortcomings of both of these tags are that they are neither interoperable nor are they compatible as they are not adhering to ISO standards. But now the organisation's current project is towards manufacturing UHF Gen 2 tags, with a Write Once Read Many tag that has larger memory (96 bits vs. 64 bits). The new EPC standard ~V Gen2 is designed with ISO standards.3[8 39]

1.6. CURRENT USES OF RFID

RFID systems have multifarious applications in various industries and for various purposes, such as tracking, identification, access management, etc. Currently, RFID is being used in such diverse areas as, product supply chain; manufacturing sector; inventory; health services; library item identification; security of organizations and vehicles; smart card technology; consumer commodity; police investigation; travel services; food and pharmaceutical tracking; motorway tolls;; animal tagging etc. Some of the applications of RFID in major areas are discussed below:

1.6.1. Apparel tracking

RFID tagging has drastically affected the apparel industry and changed the way that apparel inventory is conducted. It is dominating the scene and getting a lot of importance nowadays in achieving optimum efficiency in the inventory and management of apparels. Just by waving a hand-held electronic device thousands of garments can be located and identified within a short time. With the conventional system that made use of barcodes, it was very laborious and time consuming to do inventory check. It was very tedious to track the movement of garments on the shelves and stock rooms. But once the RFID technology is adopted, the process becomes is less laborious, less tedious and more accurate. RFID readers have the capability of providing real-time information about the exact location of a particular item and whenever an item is moved from its current location it can immediately inform the store owner of its displacement. This helps to reduce the incidences of theft in the stores. RFID tags are beneficial not just to the store owners but to consumers and shoppers as well. It could for example alert a customer when a product is out of stock.

1.6.2. Food safety and traceability

RFID technology is playing a vital role in the food processing industry by improving the, distribution, management, safety and real-time traceability of fresh foods. RFID tags are becoming popular in food processing industry for the traceability of food products from farm-to-fork chain and they enhance efficiency and accuracy in their management. This increased traceability through RFID-generated records allows food manufacturers to immediately identify and recall contaminated food products from the market if required. Furthermore, higher profitability and return on investment (ROI) can be achieved by enhanced traceability. This easier access to information leads to improved customer trust and results in higher satisfaction levels in the customers. RFID system helps in ensuring the safety, freshness and quality of food products that are transported from long distances via trains, trucks, planes, boats etc.

1.6.3. Healthcare sector

In the healthcare sector, RFID has been used in tracking patients, staff and equipment. In hospitals RFID technology can be used for the management and storing of various resources like blood samples, drugs and records of patients. RFID tagged medical equipment allows the equipment to be located dynamically, stops its theft and reduces time spent on finding assets thus leading to increased and optimum utilization of the equipments. Significant manpower savings can be achieved as the number of staff needed to search for the lost or misplaced equipment will drop significantly. Active RFID wrist band tags worn by the patients will allow them to be easily tracked across the hospital and thus restrict their movement from unwanted/restricted places. In addition, RFID tags can be used to track patient records such as their admission, discharge, prescription and transportation. RFID tag provides logistics benefit to manufacturing units in the pharmaceutical sector and electronic pedigree in their distribution units and also prevent thefts. RFID systems used for tracking and monitoring staff called the "Nurse Nanny" helps hospitals control staff cost by allowing tracking of how much time the staff members are actually spending with their patients. With the use of RFID technology, by timely intervention, it is possible to save many lives and prevent harmful situations.

1.6.4. Livestock

The worldwide market of Animal Identification is growing every year at the rate of 30%. RFID today has made it possible to identify trillions of animals such as pigs, sheep, goats, etc. Enhanced theft protection can be provided by using RFID technology that is achieved by providing each animal an encrypted unique identification. Stakeholders can improve disease control in the meat industry by updating movement data and storing vaccination information directly in the chip. This visibility to track livestock and their movements will allow governments to tax each player appropriately and provide it ability to see what is going on in the supply chain. In case of disease outbreak, the flocks that have been affected can be identified which makes it possible to withdraw the stock immediately and thus avoid unnecessary waste.

1.6.5. Passports

Beginning 2008, the US implemented the RFID-tagged passports. US Passport cards are equipped with RFID chips that store personal information and identification of the travelers in a secure government database. Passport card contains an RFID chip though it does not reveal any information about the traveler. With the help of an antenna and RFID readers installed nearby, pertinent information about the traveler such as name, age, nationality, sex, place of birth, date of birth and photograph can easily be extracted from the secure government database. This was done to maximize security on the US sea and land borders. Later many other countries have started using the RFID technology in their passports.

1.6.6. Supply chain management

For accurate identification and tracking of goods in today's retail market RFID is increasingly being used. Manufacturers, distributors and retailers are under pressure not only to maximize efficiency and provide the best possible value to the end-customer but also to minimize cost of the company. RFID is being used to manage products efficiently and cost effectively all through the chain of production, distribution and retail. By implementing RFID application in supply chains the manufacturers can especially benefit because it results in decreased costs involved in product tracking and in inventory management and its increased accuracy and timeliness. In distribution supply chain, RFID technology can be applied in monitoring the movement of the finished products and managing stock throughout the supply chain. RFID tags can be attached either directly to the materials or they can be attached to the containers that are carrying them. The cost of keeping accurate inventory data in retail can greatly be reduced with RFID application. The retailers can keep accurate inventories with fewer people and less time. The sales associates will thus be able to spend more quality time in providing service to customers rather than being involved in counting items. RFID applications in retail environments are also a significant aid in deterring thefts. Alarms are triggered when items tagged with RFID devices are removed, without being properly deactivated, from the store. RFID applications have been successfully deployed in the supply chain for several decades. It provides solutions to many operational difficulties faced if deploying any other technology or manual labor to collect data. Thus, the enterprise is able to achieve the goal of improved visibility of their products and helps them in tracking of high-value items from the source to the destination. They are enabled to reduce errors in transporting of goods to wrong destinations, results in inventory transparency, sufficient stocking of goods, improved production and smarter recalls, thereby reducing counterfeit products to a large extent.

1.6.7. Toll payment systems

Most of the road congestions are attributed to toll payment delay. Delay in toll payments can be eliminated to a great extent by application of RFID. It proves to be an effective, easier, faster and efficient toll collection solution. Antenna mounted on toll collection stations helps in identifying and classifying vehicles through the RFID enabled system. All the important information pertaining to a vehicle, such as its chassis, plate number, year model, color, body type, owner's name, franchise, late registration date, route and its engine number, etc., can be gathered through the RFID tag attached to the vehicle. Due to the elimination of toll plaza interruptions the travelers can move fast in comfort with less road congestion and traffic delay that increases customer service. RFID also guarantees assured, secured and well- managed toll collection.

Thus Radio-Frequency Identification (RFID) technology uses radio waves to read the information stored on a tag attached to an object. It is advancement on the previous bar code technology as the tag can be read from a distance of several feet and need not be within direct line-of-sight of the reader to be read. Over the previous eight decades the RFID technology has been experimented with and developed from its nascent form into the present day advanced stage. It started with the military experiments during World War II and traversed the decades to evolve into a firmly rooted and speedily expanding everyday use technology. Today it has applications in many diverse areas and has made our lives convenient. In the field of libraries RFID technology is being adopted rapidly.

2

Application of RFID in Libraries

Libraries are the nodal organisations for storing and for the dissemination of information and knowledge contained in them in the form of various documents types such as books, journals, CD-ROMs, audio-video tapes, etc. The primary purpose of any library is to provide required information to the maximum extent to its users and also make sure the optimal utilisation of the resources available in it. Hence, the libraries have been seeking aid of latest technology so as to improve their services. At present most of the libraries all over the world are using the Barcode technology to improve the efficiency of library services. Just like Barcode technology the RFID technology is also identification system that performs similar job as the barcode technology though RFID is capable of offering potentially a lot more.

According to Dictionary for Library and Information Science[40], "RFID technology is the use of microchips to tag library materials and the library card, enabling patrons to check out items by walking through a self service station equipped with an antenna that emits low- frequency radio waves. When an RF tag (transponder) passes through the electromagnetic zone, a reader (antenna + transceiver) decodes the data encoded in the tag's integrated circuit, passing it to a computer that corresponds to the library card. Line-of sight is not required for this non-contact system. RFID technology may eventually replace the barcode and optical technology in library circulation systems. Tags are available in various shapes and sizes for use in a wide range of applications, with read/write capability for interactive applications. The fact that high-frequency radio waves can be used to track moving objects at a distance has raised concerns about privacy". According to Harrod's Librarians' Glossary and Reference Book[41],"Radio Frequency Identification, an alternative to the Bar Code that uses tiny microchips in tags to hold and transmit detailed data about the item tagged. RFID has advantages over bar codes such as the ability to hold more data, the ability to change the stored data as processing occurs, it does not require line-of-sight to transfer data and is very effective in harsh environments where bar code labels may not work." Chachra (2003)[42] has described RFID "as the technology that is slated to replace barcodes in library applications". Some of the advancements of RFID system over a barcode system are that RFID tags can be used for many added purposes such as security and position control, thereby no additional security strips need to be attached to the library items. With the application of RFID technology self-checkout was made much faster and easier for the library patrons. The portable RFID scanners are capable of taking inventory by just passing them slowly along the library shelves, without the need to individually handle each item. Not only does the use of RFID save time but it operates more efficiently and effectively than the barcode system.[43]

While RFID technology by itself is not new, its application in libraries is new. Singapore Public Library is probably the first library that deployed full application of RFID technology in 1998.[44] The use of RFID by libraries over the last few years has grown dramatically. By adopting the RFID technology the libraries found a solution that made it possible for them to take the inventory of thousands of items in their collection within days instead of months. The added advantage the RFID enabled libraries have for their patrons is that it allows them to check out and return library items by themselves automatically at all times of the day. Besides speedy checkouts, the RFID technology helps in keeping the library collections in proper order and saves the librarians from repetitive strain injuries. RFID provides better theft control, reduces non-returns and chances of mis-shelving of a library's assets.

2.1. LIBRARY RFID COMPONENTS

An RFID system for library normally consists of RFID tags, a Self check-out station, a Self-return system/ Book drop system, a Staff work station, a Tagging/ Programming station, Security gate/s, a Shelf Mangement Reader / Digital Library Assistant, Conveyor belts and Sorting systems, etc.

2.1.1. RFID tag

The tag is usually flexible and thin as a paper with approx. 2" × 2" size which makes it possible for it to be inconspicuously affixed inside each book in the library collection. The tag contains an attached antenna along with a tiny chip that stores the bibliographic data of the book including its unique ID number that is used for identification of each item individually. After affixing an RFID label on a book all its individual bibliographical data including its unique identification number is stored in the chip of the tag. Information writing on chip can be done either by transferring data from the library database or by simply scanning the barcode labels if they already exist on the books, to identify each book. Active or Passive are the two types of RFID tags are available. Most of the libraries use passive tags on their collections as they have a lower cost and have an appropriate shape and size. The RFID tags can be read by the RFID gates consisting of two parallel exit sensors from a distance of up to two feet. The component of RFID used for circulation is usually called "Reader", whereas the one installed at the building exits is called "Sensor".

2.1.2. Self Check-out Station

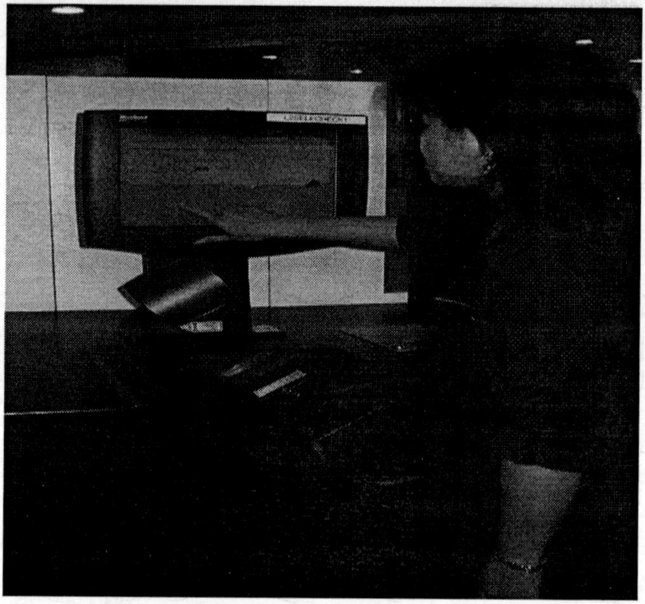

Fig. 2.1. Self-Check System (Singapore Polytechnic library)

The Self Check-out Station for the users consists of a computer with a touch screen that has an inbuilt RFID reader, is loaded with software used for reading personal identification, book identification, circulation capabilities and other required media handling. In many large libraries having considerable membership there are high volumes of circulation every day and the staff on circulation duty is many a times over burdened. With the use of RFID Self Check- out System the users are to follow the touch screen menu and they can checkout documents without going to any library staff. The library can use either RFID tag or barcode embedded user library card. When one wants to check out a document, a user puts the items selected by him on the platform of the Self Check-out unit and has to either to insert his RFID chip embedded library card in the slot of the reader or place it on the platform. The reader in turn reads the tag on the library document and transmits this information to the automated library management system. The title, accession number, author and any other optional bibliographic information is displayed on the computer screen. When the user confirms that the transaction process is complete, it generates a receipt in printed form that shows the documents that have been borrowed along with their return date. The tag on the book is then automatically deactivated or set on quiet/off so that no alarm is sounded when the checked out item passes through the exit sensors. The self-check-out station can additionally be used to verify the status of the users' account. The self-check-out station can also be modified to serve as a self-check-in station by adding a reader and a bin for the collection of the returned items. For this function the facility of generating a return receipt printout is also usually added.[45]

2.1.3. Book-drop System

The RFID book drop system consists of a book drop bin with a screen and a receipt printer. This station is very user-friendly and convenient as the users are allowed to automatically self return the library items. A reader that has been installed in a book drop unit reads the RFID tags as the user drops off the documents and automatically reactivates the security of the tag. This liberates the library staff from the laborious steps involved in check-in and reactivation of the function of security protection. The returned books and other library material go either directly to a bin or to a sorting station if one is installed. Thus the document is automatically checked- in, taken off from the library account of the user and also it reactivates the security function of the tag. Another option provided to the library in some RFID systems is that the process of return of a document will not begin until the user has inserted the user ID card. When the process completes, the user receives a printed receipt. The book drop can also be interfaced with a sorter Software. The Book-drop stations can be placed anywhere, within or outside the library. With the use of book drop system, users can return library documents at anytime of the day, on 24×7 basis.

Fig. 2.2. Book Drop System (Singapore Polytechnic library)

2.1.4. Security gates

Security gates in RFID are an Electronic Article Surveillance (EAS) system used by libraries to check thefts. The security gates have a crucial role to detect non-borrowed or improperly checked-out library items that are being out of the library. This security function is an integral feature of the chip that is contained on the RFID tag that enables it to perform both the functions of item identification and antitheft. This security feature is an integral part of the RFID tag itself and is very conveniently activated during the check-in or deactivated during the checkout operation.

Fig. 2.3. Security gates (Panjab University, Chandigarh)

The RFID exit sensors that are also called antennae and interrogators, are embedded in the security gates situated at the exit of a library, read faster and give very fewer false alarms. When a patron passes through the security gates, it reads each library document that passes between security gates and determines whether it has been properly checked-out or not and if not, then it triggers an alarm to alert the library staff. If the user ID card also has an RFID tag, the user and the checked out documents are recorded to have left the library together.

2.1.5. Automated Sorting Stations

Fig. 2.4. Automated Sorting Stations (Singapore Polytechnic library)

This component has a sophisticated sorting system that performs the functions of taking books from the return station, check them in, sort and distribute the books to multiple bins for re-shelving in different areas. Thus it enables to re-shelve the books in less time and with less staff work by determining their shelving location at the time the book is returned. Such station are required in libraries that have large circulation figures every day. It eliminates the labour intensive function of checking-in and sorting of the returned library items manually by combining a sorter device with the book drop readers. In this there are conveyers to move the returned items to the sorter.

2.1.6. Staff Work Stations

The staff work station assists the staff not only for charging and discharging library items but also for programming of new library documents, sorting of library documents, etc. The workstation has two parts i.e. a reader and a PC. For programming or tagging of a new library document with the help of staff workstation, the document is first placed on the reader, the accession number of the document is read with a barcode scanner and then the data associated with that particular accession number is downloaded from the library management system. By linking this to the RFID tag it is programmed. Staff work station is used for multiple purposes: editing and updating of user's record by addition and deletion; can generate borrowing history of a particular user; delay fine management; activating and deactivating of Electronic Article Surveillance chip inside the library documents; programming of new library documents; sorting of library documents according to their area and call number.

Fig. 2.5. Staff workstations (SVNIT Library, Gujarat)[46]

2.1.7. Tagging and programming station

The RFID tags affixed to the library items are programmed at the programming station. If the item is already affixed with a barcode the barcode is read using a standard barcode scanner and its associated data is automatically transferred to the tag of the book placed on the programming station. In case the book is not already bar-coded, a self adhesive RFID tag is pasted on the book and it is placed on the programming station that is already connected to a PC. The accession number associated with that particular book is keyed in and the bibliographic data of the book is transferred from the library management system to the tag. The tag is thus said to have been programmed. RFID programming station consists of two components i.e. an RFID reader and an antenna. This station can not only read the information stored on the RFID tag but also update the RFID tag with revised or additional information. It is capable of this due to the application software it holds that has been specifically designed for this required task. A programming station is also known as a conversion station, a programmer, a tagging station, or reader-writer. It can transfer the unique identification number of an item to an RFID tag either by using key board of a PC or by scanning a barcode. Portable carts can also be used as programming stations to facilitate conversion in the stack areas.

Fig. 2.6. Tagging and Programming Station (SVNIT Library, Gujrat)[46]

2.1.8. Portable Reader

A portable RFID reader is used for inventory and shelf reading. The reader functions by transmitting the unique identification number of the item to the server, which in turn sends this information to the library management software and a quick response is received in real time. The other way is to download the information with library management software for inventory control. This Shelf Management system helps the librarians in locating and identifying items lying on the shelves easy. A handheld reader makes other shelf- management activities like weeding out, finding missing items and out-of-order books quick and easy work. The handheld reader comprises of a portable scanner and a base station. This is generally used to search for a particular book that has been requested, for inventory check of the library stock and to rectify the shelf arrangement of books.

Fig. 2.7. Digital Library Assistant (University of East London, UK)

To perform these functions the portable scanner is swept across the spines of the books that are affixed with RFID tags lying on the shelves. For stock taking purposes, the data collected through the reader is compared with the library management system database and then generate a discrepancy report. In situations where search function is required for a particular document, the information of that document at first is transferred from the base station into a portable scanner and when it is swept across the shelves if a similar document is found, a built-in beeper sounds to alert the librarian.[47]

2.1.9. Application software

The reader transmits from or receives data from a tag by using the application software. The hardware of the reader is also integrated with the existing Library Automation Software being used by the library by using this software, so as to allow smooth functioning of the circulation section. In the barcode technology the information once stored on the barcode initially cannot be reprogrammed but once the RFID technology is implemented not only information storage capacity can be increased, but reprogramming facility can also be provided. All the parameters of the library i.e. its users, books and periodicals can be integrated by using the RFID system so as to extend various applications that are integrated with the library automation system. General applications are integrated with the peripherals and the middleware controls the automation system and the RFID system. The middleware provides the Automation systems also known as Application Interfaces (API) that are used for communication with RFID readers and through them the information stored on the tags is accessed.

2.1.10. Server

A server is a component of the RFID system that is loaded with the software that acts as an interface with the integrated library management software. The server can be said to be the heart of the RFID system. The various components of the RFID system communicate through the server thus it acts as a communication gateway. The server when it receives the information from the readers exchanges it with the circulation database. The software loaded on the server includes the Applications Programming Interface (APIs) to enable it to interface with the automated library management system. The server can produce reports as it includes a transaction database.[48]

2.2. LIBRARY RFID STANDARDS AND PROTOCOLS

2.2.1. ISO 15693

It is an international standard that deals with the interface between the software in the readers and the tags. It defines the air interface, the communication protocol and the physical characteristics for RFID tags. It operates at a frequency of 13.56 MHz and allows the read distance of 1.5 meters (approx. 59 inches) maximum between the tag and the reader. Mostly the RFID applications used in libraries conform to this standard. However, the design of this standard was for container level tracking and not for the item-level tracking that is required by libraries.

2.2.2. ISO-18000-3

This is an international standard that governs the read/write passive tags that operate at a frequency of 13.56 MHZ and have a range limited to 24 inches. The RFID tags used in libraries conform to this standard. The vendor of RFID technology decides upon the data blocks on the tags and their number and function. This standard provides the facility of item level tracking, however, it has a drawback that it does not provide interoperability amongst the tags of different companies

2.2.3. ISO 28560

It is a three-part international standard released in the year 2011 and is essentially used for making RFID systems interoperable. The format of RFID tags for use in the library system is provided by this standard. The part 1 of the standard describes specifically the date elements and the data models, while part 2 and part 3 provide the two options for encoding the data to be stored on the tags. Most of the libraries globally have adopted one of these standards to ensure interoperability among tags.

2.2.4. SIP2 (Standard Interchange Protocol)

These are the standards developed by 3M for the

user self-charging station and RFID system to enable communication with the integrated library management system. By using this standard one can determine if the person using the system is a valid borrower and also to make sure none of the library defined limits on borrowing are violated or exceeded. After thorough checking the check-out or check-in information is passed between the RFID reader and the integrated library management system.

2.2.5. NCIP (NISO Circulation Interchange Protocol)

This standard is gradually replacing SIP2. It has been designed specifically to support communication between the RFID system and an integrated library management system. The NCIP protocol was formulated specifically for four application areas: self-service, direct consortia borrowing, circulation/interlibrary loan interchange and access to electronic resources.[49]

2.3. HOW RFID SYSTEM WORKS IN THE LIBRARY

Fig. 2.8. Library RFID Management Systems[50]

The RFID technology works through, paper- thin flexible RFID tags, that are inconspicuously placed on the inside of front or back cover of each document in the collection of a library including collections like CDs, DVDs, etc. Complete information about each and every item in the collection is entered into the Library Management Software. When a user desires to issue or return a document, the RFID reader reads the information from the tag, affixed on it and transmits the data to the software and the book is seamlessly issued in a very short time say a few seconds without any intervention required manually. As the user goes out of the library with the issued book, the antennae placed in the exit security gates automatically read the information stored on the RFID tag and verify if the book has been properly issued or not. In case the book is not issued to a valid user as per library norms or if it is being stolen from the library, the antennae in the exit gate sense it and sound an instant alarm. In this way the deployment RFID technology results in successful reduction of theft of books and other items from the library. The RFID technology can also be effectively used for stock taking and other library management practices.

2.4. ISSUES RELATED TO USE OF RFID IN LIBRARIES

2.4.1. Privacy

Due to their nature RFID tags are vulnerable to privacy breach as unauthorised scanners may read the information stored on the tags. To offset this concern most RFID tags used in libraries contain a minimum amount of information in fact essentially the same information as contained on the barcodes. But even though the tag may contain nothing more than a unique identification number as in a bar code, there are privacy concerns. Molner & Wagner (2010)[51] have highlighted the potential threats of implementing RFID to patron privacy that include unauthorised tags reading, writing, hotlisting, eavesdropping and tracking. Unauthorised tag reading occurs when the unencrypted data is transmitted between the reader and tag, making it easily vulnerable to being read by an unauthorised reader. Unauthorised tag writing happens when an unauthorised reader inserts data onto the tag during the normal process of read-write. As an example, an unauthorised reader could reset the security bit illegally, thus allowing the user to walk out of the library with an unchecked-out book. In the process of Hotlisting the illegally captured data from the tag is matched with a specifically targeted item. Eventually an illegal database of tag codes could be built up and the title of the item associated with each tag can be distorted. Tracking is the process of using the tag affixed on the book to keep track of the movements and location of an individual. However, for tracking to be effective, the individual being tracked must carry the tagged books and there must be unauthorised readers wherever the person travels.

2.4.2. Cost

While there are many benefits of RFID, the cost of the same is high. For implementing RFID system in Indian libraries, the approximate cost of RFID system includes - RFID tags which varies from Rs. 11-22 each, Security gates which are in the range of Rs. 4,00000- 5,00000, Staff Work station which is in the range of Rs. 1,45,000- 2,00000, Installation & Commissioning of RFID system which varies from Rs. 50,000- 1,00000, Application Software in the range of Rs. 2,00,000- 2,50,000, Server/ Docking Station which may cost around Rs. 3,00000- Self Check Station in the range of Rs. 4,50,000- 5,00000, Book-Drop Kiosk in the range of Rs. 5,25,000- 5,75,000, Portable RFID reader (Digital Library Assisnat) in the range of Rs. 2,25,000- 2,50,000, etc.[52]

2.4.3. Vulnerability to compromise

There is a possibility of compromising an RFID system by wrapping the RFID protected and tagged items in two or three layers of ordinary household foil. By such wrapping the radio signal of the tag will be blocked and the antennae of the security gates will not be able to detect them. Obviously, if someone brings household foil into a library that uses RFID technology it would definitely be a premeditated theft, similar to the case of bringing a magnet into a library using EM technology would be. Another way to compromise an RFID enabled system is to place two RFID tagged items against one another in a way so that the tags substantially cover each other by overlaying. In this way the two overlaying tags shall cancel the each other's radio signals. However this would require a good knowledge of the technology and substantial care in overlaying the tags.[53]

2.4.4. Removal of exposed tags

RFID tags used on books cannot be concealed in a very effective way as they cannot be fixed either in the spine or gutter of the books. Tags are typically affixed to the inside back cover of a book and are easily visible and thus exposed to being removed by anyone. Even if the library wishes to fix the RFID tags in the spine of books they are not flexible enough to be inserted in thc spines. However, if a library wishes it can imprint the RFID tags with its logo which will then make the tags appear like book plates used on the library collection or a printed label cover or plain page can be pasted over each tag.54

2.4.5. Exit sensor problems

The short-range readers used for circulation i.e. for activation and deactivation of tags and for inventory control can read the tags 100 percent, but the performance of the exit sensors on the security gates is more problematic, it is not 100 percent most of the time. They should be able to read tags at up to twice the distance of that of the other readers. The exit sensors function better when the antennae on the tags are larger or when the exit gates are not more than 36 to 42 inches wide.[55]

2.4.6. Standards

There are no real agreed international standards world-wide for RFID systems. This hinders the adoption of the technology in many areas and creates issues in interoperability. Only set frequency bands and some guidelines are available with regards to RFID. Operational standards and regulations vary from country to country.

Thus we can rightly conclude that the RFID technology has ample scope to make the services and management of libraries efficient and effective and save the time of the user as well as help the librarians to perform their functions easily. It can liberate the library staff from laborious manual work so as to enable them to contribute more efficiently in providing other meaningful services to the users. It definitely improves the usefulness of the library and increases user satisfaction levels. With the formulation of international standards the RFID technology has a wider and more regulated market now. Interoperability of components enables libraries to add RFID technology in the areas that they initially didn't cater for or didn't have the budget for.

However, like every new technology the RFID technology also has its shortcomings. There are some areas that are of concern to libraries such as the issue of privacy of personal data and being susceptible to compromise. Libraries have to implement it cautiously and with proper checks.

3

Adoption of RFID in Libraries: An Evolutionary Study through Literature

When any new technology is evolved it takes advantage of the knowledge that has accumulated over the years as a result of constant research. Review of the related literature helps the user to acquaint oneself with current knowledge in the field. The available literature was searched for the purpose and books, journals, dissertations, reports, databases, e-documents, the Internet on use of RFID technology in libraries and information centers, were explored. To understand the importance of RFID technology in libraries various reviews that emphasize the benefits and problems in the implementation of RFID in libraries need to be studied. As revealed by the results obtained from the Scopus Citation database as well as the Web of Science, no literature was available in the field application of RFID in libraries prior to 2000. Whatever literature is available prior to 2000, dealt with application of RFID in areas other than libraries such as mining, logistics, aviation, etc. The literature related to RFID use in libraries is as follows:

3.1. RFID USE IN LIBRARIES WORLD WIDE

3.1.1. 2001-2005

Chia[56] in his paper reported a need to transform the present library system of Singapore as was strongly recommended by the National Library Board. This was to influence four main areas in libraries i.e., content, services, people and infrastructure. He believed that the transformation of libraries in Singapore could be possible only with by properly implementing the recommendations of NLB. He claims that NLB was the first in the world to launch an Electronic Library Management System (ELiMS). It took not more than 15 minutes waiting to borrow library material during peak hours and zero waiting time to return book. He claimed using ELiMS, stocktaking of books in a library would take less than a day, which used to take two weeks earlier. NLB and its technology partners were awarded the International Certificate of Grant of Patent in December 2000 for RFID applications in tracking and monitoring of books. He has enumerated the achievements of the NLB since 1995. NLB is a key player in the nation's learning enterprise and has fulfilled many of the strategies outlined in the Library 2000 Report.

In the year 2001 Yorkovich[57] studied the use of 3M Digital ID (Digital Library Assistant). He stated that its use streamlined the processing of library material and saved the time of library staff that was previously being used up on performing routine functions such as searching for lost items, weeding out the old library collection, proper shelving of items, performing shelf reading etc. These functions could now be performed in a fraction of the time spent earlier. He felt that with the use of 3M Self Check System, Lied Library patrons could now issue out the desired library material themselves, without the intervention of the library staff. The RFID system could read information from the digital identification tag and could process both bar-coded and digital identification items and it required no line of sight. According to his opinion DLA was the most revolutionary technology that affected the way libraries managed information and with its use, a library's efficiency to retrieve information is enhanced.

Yuan et al.[58] (2002) claimed that Singapore was the first in the world to use RFID system in the libraries so that the users could borrow and return books by themselves at their own convenience, by bypassing the human librarian. They proposed using an intelligent robotic book retrieval and return system with RFID tags. They observed that isolated robotic system is only capable of shelving and retrieving the books that are located in the shelves up to a height of 2m. They recommended 13.56 MHz frequency system for isolated robotic system and concluded that intelligent robotic system with the ability to identify books can be suitably implemented with RFID system.

Fabbi et al.[59] in 2002 in their article discussed the various components of an RFID technology and its assimilation and testing at a branch library of UNLV, the Curriculum Materials Library (CML). The challenges faced and the implementation differences between a small and large library are outlined in this article. The authors predicted both the future growth for product and use of the system in UNLV libraries. They observed that after the implementation of 3M Digital Identification System at UNLV libraries, performance and efficiency of the library staff had increased many fold and users had also benefited in several ways. They could independently check out library materials and found the books properly arranged on the shelves which was made possible with the use of the Digital Library Assistant. They concluded that implementation of RFID system at the UNLV libraries changed the way the staff managed their work and Performed the library tasks.

Ngian[60] in 2003 in his paper discussed the implementation of the Totally Do-It-Yourself (DIY) concept in the National Library of Singapore. He reported in his study that after the implementation of RFID, the library was able to automate almost fully its circulation service functions such as the payment of overdue fines and fees through a national cash card; online and real-time checking of loan account and registration of new members etc. He reported that on the first day of the opening of the library equipped with the new technology, more than 12,300 people visited and they borrowed 13,900 items. 128 new members registered themselves and 255 enquiries were made using the Cybrarian service. The Totally DIY library was developed as a prototype by the National Library Board (NLB) of Singapore. The NLB planned to implement this concept in a few other libraries though not in all of its 22 libraries. This interesting and exciting concept was found to reduce the operating cost and extended opening hours of libraries where there was a need, was now possible.

Kern[61] in his article in 2004 stated that RFID system was already being used in UNLV library in USA. It had application in areas of self- checkout, theft control, inventory taking and for sorting and conveying of library books and other materials. He noted that the application of RFID in these areas of library services were expected to result in significant cost savings in terms of labour; it would enhance customer satisfaction; reduce incidents of book theft and provide a constantly update record of collections. The components and technical features of a modern RFID library system were described by him and he also provided guidelines for evaluating the different systems. He prepared a short report on the basis of installations in three European institutions (one university library and two public libraries). With the availability of new generation of RFID-chips ISO standard 15693 in the market he stated that non-proprietary system could now be used in the library systems.

Kern and Nauer[62] in 2004 surveyed over 20 RFID enabled libraries in Switzerland and observed that more than 90% library visitors could easily be guided to use the RFID stations installed in libraries. The study showed that Vienna public library about 60% readers used the self-checkout stations. In their study they reported there were two main factors that were relevant for the introduction of the RFID technology in libraries, i.e. reduction in the cost of the technology and the availability of international standards. They revealed in the study that cost of 100,000 labels came down more than 50% within a year i.e. from 2003 to 2004 from 1.20 EUR to 0.50 EUR. This became possible due to the increased application of RFID technology in other industry sectors such as logistics, personnel identification etc. The RFID technology was becoming cost effective as investment cost was reducing and accordingly becoming affordable for more libraries. They also provided recommendations for the allocation of functional units of RFID in a library.

Sheck[63], in order to handle the increased volume of circulation, using the same number of staff, Seattle Public Library invested in RFID to automate check in and sort returns. He highlighted various advantages of using RFID technologies for such functions as automated check-in/check-out of library materials, automated sorting of returned documents, security of library collections, etc. He concluded that without such technology, it would be very difficult for the Seattle Public Library staff to keep up with all the new services.

In another study in the same year Molnar and Wagner[64] described the current deployments and suggested novel architecture for library RFID. The prevalent traditional knowledge suggested that privacy risks were negligible unless someone unauthorised has access to library databases. They contradicted this assumption in their study. The key technical issue identified by them was private authentication, i.e., they wondered how a reader and a tag could authenticate each other without revealing their identities to an adversary. They proposed a general scheme for building private authentication with work algorithm in the tags and proposed a scheme of linear work as a sub-protocol. They also suggested a simple scheme without any complicated heavy cryptography that would guard against a passive adversary using XOR alone. They found that more than 130 libraries in North America had installed RFID technology and many more were planning to. They suggested careful designing of the entire system and supported privacy-enabled RFID applications. They concluded that the American Library Association should propose the best practices for the library use of RFID as a result the adoption rate of the technology would rise dramatically.

In the year 2005 Rafiq[65] presented an in depth study of RFID uses in libraries with a roadmap of its implementation, the impact of RFID on library services, and also a comparison of major vendors and their products. He has presented a detailed study of RFID technology, its components, how it works, and its utility in various sectors, i.e., supply chains, livestock industry, courier services, logistics, wireless transactions and especially in libraries. He stated that RFID has revolutionized the working of various industries and services of institutions by increasing their efficiency, and improving profitability. He is of the opinion that RFID is how inexpensive and it can make surveillance increasingly online in this interconnected world. One of the major concerns of privacy of organizations such as the Electronic Frontier Foundation (EFF) is the possibility of remotely tracking people with their RFID tags. He concluded that patron satisfaction has become crucial for librarians. Most of the libraries are planning to implement RFID technology as it has proven to bring convenience and efficiency in item management and made possible the automation of workflow.

In 2005 Fabbi et al.[66] studied the system hardware and software activities and developments at the UNLV libraries related to the 3M™ Digital Materials

Flow Management. They highlighted the benefits of using Digital Library Assistant in UNLV libraries and stated that the major benefit of using the DLA is that it is able to do shelf reading while simultaneously collecting inventory data in the background. Another important benefit is that after initially scanning and shelf-reading the complete library collection with the help of DLAs, problem books in the library could be identified. Some of the issues with these problem books could be easily solved such as errors in cataloguing data, incorrect call number labels, missing or long-lost items, books that had no item record, and items that were lying on the shelf but were shown as still checked out to patrons. They also found out that with the use of the 3M™ Digital Materials Flow Management system, the UNLV libraries were able to form more efficient norms for undertaking collection management activities, such as inventory control and weeding out of unserviceable books, increased level of user satisfaction that resulted from an accurate shelf order, convenient checkout by the users and the enhanced ability to find items that were long since presumed to be missing. However, they cautioned that as technology progressed the libraries must continually assess RFID systems and keep a close watch on the issue of patron privacy. Additionally the possibilities from further collaboration between libraries and vendors in the area and developments arising from them such as product standardization were expected.

In the same year i.e. 2005 Karen[67] in her article described the use of RFID in library circulation and inventory function. She opined that any new technology added has to be measured by "Return on Investment" or ROI and satisfaction level of the users. These are the two most important measures of success of any technology. Although she stated that RFID is not a highly secure technology she felt that this technology cannot be ignored even if libraries are using it today or not, they have to think of using it in the future.

Dawes[68] in his article in the year 2005 entitled "Is RFID right for your library?" stated that libraries are implementing RFID technology at an increasingly rapid pace. He studied the benefits and shortcomings of RFID technology for libraries. He opined that though the number of libraries employing this technology at that point of time was few, the benefits of the technology cannot be ignored. He enumerated the advantages to libraries, which were considering implementing RFID. They need to consider the increased circulation speed, better inventory control, and returns with sorting capabilities. However, he concluded that ultimately it is an individual choice of each library. Each library needs to perform its own cost benefit analysis before implementing it.

During the period 2001-2005 the libraries all over the world had started to think about using the RFID technology in the libraries, though very few libraries had actually started using the technology. The benefits and drawbacks of the technology in the libraries were being considered and researched from the cost benefit point of view.

3.1.2. 2006-2010

In 2006 Hopkinson and Chandrakar69 in their study titled "Introducing RFID at Middlesex University Learning Resource" discussed problems associated with the installation and use of RFID in Middlesex University. They shared that on the very first day that the renovated library was opened to users, the library encountered a problem of database, as the hardware running the university firewall failed. As a result no user could log in to the library management system. However, they observed that self-checkout and self-return systems became very popular with the users in no time and 64 per cent of issues and returns were done using the system. Due to the RFID technology, the number of hours that the staff is engaged in circulation work and stock management also reduced. They drew the conclusion that with the introduction of RFID, the library services had become more user-friendly.

Another author Palmer[70] in 2006 in an article entitled "Using RFID to transform Essex libraries" stated that in order to transform libraries in twenty-first century into modern institutions and to increase users satisfaction, in Essex the libraries have implemented RFID technology. He stated that initially the libraries around the world were rather hesitant to use the RFID technology but after a rather slow beginning it took off fairly rapidly. He claimed that with less than 50 libraries in late 2001 using the technology, the estimates suggested that the number rose to around 500 libraries by October 2005. The reason for its increasing popularity was that RFID offered not just a solution to the security aspect, but also offered the possibility of self service and stock taking facility that was not available in the traditional method. He found that RFID self service had become popular with library users and had brought about significant changes to the library services being offered. The ease of use of self-service was the main reason that accounted for approximately 50 percent of total transactions being done through the RFID system. However, he felt that implications in stock management needed further exploration.

Singh et al[71] in their article in 2006 titled "The state of RFID applications in libraries" stated that with the adoption of RFID technology by libraries they could inventory hundreds of thousands of items in their collection in days which earlier took them months to do.

In addition, it had the advantage of allowing the users to automatically check out and return library property at any time of the day without any limitation of time. They were of the opinion that with the use of RFID technology not only the checkouts were speeded up, but it was also possible to keep the library collections in proper order. It helped in avoiding repetitive strain injuries among librarians, controlled theft of items, non returns, and misfiling of the library's items. They surveyed twenty nine libraries to investigate the state of RFID applications in them and reported that out of them only ten had migrated to the RFID based system. Of the remaining nineteen libraries under survey, thirteen had already started the process of migrating to RFID. For a library the average conversion cost to migrate to an RFID system was quite high. 50% of the participating libraries showed that there was more than 10% increase in usage after the implementation of RFID. The two most-installed or sought after components of the RFID system noted by them were the patron self-checkout and the staff conversion stations. They concluded that though RFID tags were costlier by four to five times than the barcodes and magnetic strips combined, an increasing number of libraries were considering to implement this technology due to the increase in efficiency and functionality provided by RFID.

In 2007 Shamsudin et al.[72] in their article titled "RFID-based intelligent books shelving system" observed the most difficult task often carried out by the library personnel was the searching of misplaced books and found that it was practically difficult to place all books back in their assigned locations on a daily basis. With the use of RFID based intelligent shelving system, books management monitoring can be done efficiently through wireless communication between the RFID reader and the book. With the help of RFID based intelligent shelving system the library staff could now easily place all the library books at the right location with minimum time and effort involved. They further discussed the performance efficiency of RFID reader and tags data management and their proficiency in retrieving information, matching it with database, sorting out in order and displaying the status of library items. They concluded that the performance of the RFID based intelligent shelving system is satisfactory and it has a potential ability to alleviate the labour intensive efforts involved in shelving books.

In the same year Curtin et al[73] in their research work entitled "Making the most out of RFID technology: a research agenda for the study of the adoption, usage and impact of RFID" observed that RFID technology could drastically increase the ability of an organization to acquire a wide variety of data about the location and properties of any physically tagged entity that can be wirelessly scanned within certain technical limitations. They opined that RFID had a variety of applications in tasks, structures, work systems and contexts in the value chain, that included logistics, internal operations, consumer marketing and after-sales service etc. As there is wider adoption of RFID in industry, scholarly investigation by academic researchers to understand how RFID relates to Mobility, Organizational and Systems Technologies (MOST) was increased. They addressed a series of research questions related to how to adopt and implement RFID technology by organizations, what are its uses, how it is evolved and supported within the organizations and mainly its impact in business industries and markets.

Again in 2007 Shien-Chiang[74] in his paper "RFID implementation and benefits in libraries" built a model for implementing RFID technology in libraries. He opined that RFID applications are better than barcodes as they could provide batch access, mass data storage and the option of reprogramming. He pointed out that one of the major factors hindering the adoption of RFID in libraries was the cost involved. He studied the feasibility of the structure and application of the RFID system. He concluded that to economize on the expense, initially RFID should be applied to particular collections and later on extended to other collections.

In the same year Kevin and Martin[75] wrote an article entitled "A primer on Radio Frequency Identification for libraries". In this they stated that RFID is basically a location determining technology that had generated a lot of commercial attention recently, especially for asset tracking and in supply chain management. They discussed a library RFID prototype that utilised the technology for faster book search and identification process. They identified the hardware required to design and implement the prototype which included a laptop that would host the server, a router to create the wireless network, a PDA to host the applications, RFID tags and an RFID reader for communication. The functionality and benefits that the RFID system offered matched the needs of users and could be used in the areas of libraries that needed improvement. They observed that RFID technology can improve major library functions such as book searching and stock taking. They reported that only approximately 8 per cent of libraries world over were making use of RFID technology. The evaluation of library application of RFID has demonstrated that it can be successfully integrated into library systems so as to improve the efficiency of any library and enhance the quality of services provided by them. They opined that RFID has the ability to uniquely identify each and every item that makes it quite suitable for use in libraries.

Potdar et al[76] in 2007 in their paper "Improving RFID read rate reliability by a systematic error detection approach" addressed the issues of reliability in general and read rate failures detection in particular. They studied the issues involved in the detection of RFID tags, why they are not read and if the tags are not read an alarm should be activated. This issue is quite different from the current RFID reliability research which mainly attempted to increase the read rate by developing new and powerful antennas or concentrated on improving the surrounding environment. They found out a solution so as the missed readings can be detected and appropriate entity can be notified so that suitable action against it can be taken. The unique feature of the proposed solution was the combined use of RFID reader and a normal weighing machine. In this concept the gross weight of the tagged items is compared with the gross weight of the same item stored in a backend database. Their observation was that the backup database could only be accessed for those RFID tags that were read properly. The weights of the tags that are not read at all would vary and hence incorrect readings could be identified. They gave a detailed theoretical foundation for the solution they proposed. They also compared their proposed solution with the existing solutions available so as to demonstrate its success and its potential for practical use in a library or in the supermarket.

Gómez-Gómez et al.[77] in the same year i.e. 2007 their article entitled "RFID in library management and maintenance" stated that RFID is currently growing in importance. They explained that libraries can improve inventory control and track library items by gathering data from RFID labels on the library collection. They revealed that most of the libraries use RFID of 13.56 MHz or less and are following ISO 15693 and 18000-3 standards. They described the components and operation of an RFID system and applications in diverse sectors particularly with respect to libraries. They proposed a general RFID implementation model for the libraries and practical applications currently in use along with benefits like faster issue return, inventory control, etc.

In the year 2007 So and Liu[78] in their article "Learning from failure: a case study of adopting Radio Frequency Identification technology in library services" said that the RFID technology can improve customer satisfaction and service efficiency and that is the reason why it is widely used in many business organisations. They focused on issues in its implementation and formulated strategies to tackle the problems encountered. They analysed the pros and cons of adopting RFID technology in a medium-sized library. They were of the opinion that for successful implementation of any technology in an organisation there are many factors, and out of them the organisation's readiness is the most important. The preparedness of people, strategy, processes and system maturity should be ensured before going in for the technology and for it to be successful.

Muir[79] in 2007 in his paper "RFID security concerns" noted that a large number of libraries had started implementing RFID technology with solutions either supplementing or replacing the existing barcode systems. He was apprehensive that while RFID technology offered many advantages over the other technologies, it also had a downside that there is a probability of exposing libraries and their users to potential violations of privacy both internally and externally. He was of the opinion that RFID warrants further review in view of an escalating, ongoing debate over libraries and patron privacy in the present era. He studied if these concerns were genuine and suggested best practices and recommended measures to minimize the privacy risks to libraries and their patrons. He wanted that any library implementing the RFID system should be aware of the potential risks associated with RFID technology and security violations that are a potential threat to the users.

Butters[80] in 2007 in his paper "RFID systems, standards and privacy within libraries" discussed the RFID standards which were currently being used in the libraries and found out that only two mainly used standards in the RFID solutions currently available to libraries are: ISO/ IEC 15693 and ISO/IEC 18000-3 Mode 1 and both of these cannot provide a truly secure RFID architecture. He suggested a list of steps to be taken to protect the privacy of library users, like not to use RFID tags on borrower cards, the amount of data on each RFID tag should be reduced, not allow the public to perform bibliographic searches by using the barcode, etc. He stressed on the training of library staff and users so that they can accurately assess the actual risk factors. He concluded that RFID systems have several vulnerabilities and the current standards do not offer a secure platform. Every library has to make their own decision of migration to RFID keeping in view the risks/benefits involved and must ensure that the users are aware of the project and any security concerns that borrowers might have are resolved.

Butters[81] in the year 2008 in his paper "RFID in Australian academic libraries: exploring the barriers to implementation" stated that RFID technology is evolving at a rapid pace and being increasingly adopted by business and other organisations the world over, especially in the Asia Pacific region. He has stated the advantages of implementing RFID technology in libraries and suggested a number of factors that contributed to the lack of popularity of the technology in the Australian academic library sector. He said that since 2002, RFID system has been installed in a large number of Australian libraries including public, school and special libraries and found that there were some positive implications of implementing RFID, such as increased productivity, occupational safety and health and collection management.

In 2008 Butter[82] in his paper "RFID for libraries: a comparison of high frequency and ultra high frequency options" stated that almost all libraries today function with High Frequency (HF) RFID tags and readers, that internationally operate at a frequency of 13.56 Mh. However, RFID technology is continuously evolving and there may be other technological options also that may be used as the basis for library RFID system. He prophesied that UHF technology is the future basis for library RFID applications because of its low cost and better performance as compared to HF tags.

Yu[83] in 2008 in his article "Implementation of an innovative RFID application in libraries" described the Shih-Hsin University Library's RFID system that uses UHF and has long distance induction to assist in innovative applications. The basic three applications of RFID are local searching and positioning for collections and correct the mis-shelving or find items lost in library, statistics calculation in terms of usage frequency and length of time of book reading and instant library guidance service. He deducted that RFID can replace barcodes and magnetic strips to provide for better security control and collection management. The library can provide innovative library services, i.e., searching and positioning, measuring access and reading rate, provide information for location of library collections, etc. with the use of RFID. He concluded that with the implementation of RFID service efficiency of libraries is improved. However, it was necessary to regulate standards, processes, and interfaces and continuous efforts are required to extend automatic library operations.

In 2007 Golding and Tennant84 in their article "Performance testing: evaluating an RFID library inventory reader" examined the operational efficiencies of the inventory reader and the self-check station. They pointed out that a number of studies had been done in supply chain scenario to determine the performance requirement so as to achieve 100% read rate. However, they found that sparse literature on testing of RFID in the library environment is available. They carried out a survey at a university library and conducted a sample test of 200 books of different types. The factors they examined were placement of tags, sensitivity of reader orientation, read distance and other possible sources of electromagnetic interference such as metal etc. Their findings confirmed that mobile devices and wireless computers do not interfere in the performance of the self-check station or inventory reader. However, the preliminary results suggested that it is the metallic shelves that affect the performance of the inventory reader and reduce the read rate accuracy.

Golding and Tennant[85] in 2008 in their article "Evaluation of a Radio Frequency Identification (RFID) library system: preliminary results" studied an academic library that had a fully implemented RFID system and with a collection of approximately 120,000 tagged books. They studied operational issues of RFID that relate to performance of the inventory reader and self check station so that optimal accuracy rate can be achieved. The test sample taken consisted of 200 books of varying sizes that included both paper back and hard cover. For each, test sample readings were taken and recorded 40 times. They noted that the books that were the closest to the metal separator or to the metal upright were consistently misread. These books had to be physically removed from the shelves to obtain a correct reading. They also reported that there was no observable effect or interference in the performance of self-check station and RFID transmission and reception with the use of cell phone, computers and laptop.

In the same year Lau et al[86] in their paper "A smart bookshelf for library RFID system" presented the novel idea of a smart book shelf for libraries that use a UHF RFID system, that was installed with their self designed RFID system including readers, antennas and self developed software. They performed field tests on UHF RFID system at their original location according to various performance indicators like read range, speed, read rate etc. They concluded that with the help of a UHF RFID system based smart shelf, the user can locate the books easily within few minutes with the use of the friendly RFID interface.

Ching and Tai[87] in 2009 in their paper "HF RFID versus UHF RFID-Technology for library service transformation at City University of Hong Kong" noted that the City University of Hong Kong started the UHF RFID pilot test in April 2008. Since the implementation of this pilot project the check-outs of the library collection increased by 50%. They stated that throughout the pilot test, as reported by the UHF RFID application no item was misread. According to their study the performance of UHF RFID tags of the security gates was much superior to HF tags and they concluded that UHF tags outperformed HF tags in terms of reading rate, detection rate of multiple-items, and read range for self-check machines and the security gates.

In 2009 Robkin[88] in his article "Managing multivendor RFID rollouts" stated that with operational budgets of libraries being cut down all over the world, many libraries are adopting RFID system to track their inventories and to manage the working of circulation, thereby reducing operating cost and increasing efficiency. He discussed the implementation of RFID in the Jessamine County Public Library's (USA) and reported that patrons and staff members benefit from its implementation. He suggested that before implementing RFID, a series of trial and error is required for a week before all settings are just right. He also suggested that training of library staff is essential for maintenance and troubleshooting to diagnose problems quickly and efficiently. He emphasised that the crux of a successful multivendor system would be to choose compatible vendors, develop a communication strategy and establish clear procedures for troubleshooting.

Bahri[89] in 2010 in his article "Enhancing the delivery of library's services through the implementation of an emerging information technology: a process framework" presented a procedural framework for the implementation of this emerging information technology in library. He developed a framework to identify the key process of implementation of RFID into three stages: unfreezing, moving and refreezing. During the unfreezing stage one needs to form a partnership between the librarian and the vendor. During the moving stage, several issues emerged which included linking the RFID system to the library's LMS, RFID tagging process, resistance of staff, etc. During refreezing stage, it must be ensured that the system is up-to-date according to the latest standards. Only if the system is up-to-date, the library can think of extending the RFID applications or adding more RFID-based applications in the library. He further suggested that the library needs to address technical issues with the vendor and vendor has to be a partner all the time so as to resolve any technical issues that may crop up immediately. He emphasised that a library has to deal efficiently with any resistance from the staff. He concluded that once the RFID system has been installed, the library staff must receive proper training on how to use the system.

In 2010 Blansit[90] in his article "RFID terminology and technology: preparing to evaluate RFID for your library" was of the opinion that libraries can use RFID without appreciable privacy concerns. He studied that there was no privacy issue in use of RFID system in libraries because a user cannot determine information about any of the items from the RFID tag, if he does not have access to the library automation system. He said that with a proper understanding of the underlying principles of RFID technology commonly used in libraries the librarian will be helped in investigating and identifying the possible uses of RFID within a library.

Caldwell-Stone[91] in 2010 in his paper "RFID in libraries" reviewed the controversial situation arisen due to the use of RFID technology in U.S. libraries and the steps taken by the library professionals for the resolution of those issues. He studied the privacy issues and the recommendations that the NISO's RFID Working Group made for use in U.S. libraries. He opined that best practices for use of RFID in the libraries should be developed that would not only facilitate use of the technology but would also promote the distinctive mission of the library. The privacy rights of the users' must be preserved. He cautioned that while standards and practices recommended can be easily revised and re-written to accommodate new RFID applications, but if the privacy is once lost it cannot be recovered easily. He recommended that data models for best practices and standards for RFID applications in libraries must be established, interoperability between library RFID applications should be ensured and the librarian should play a major role in ensuring privacy of data both inside and outside the library, as it is a their ethical obligation to protect library users' privacy. He drew the conclusion that the standards developed for RFID should make privacy protection the major goal and not just a secondary goal.

In 2010 Cunningham[92] in his study entitled "A case study into the implementation of RFID at the Pilkington Library Loughborough University" studied and found that most of the library users gave a positive feedback about the new system and that 91% of the patrons used the new technology in the very first year of its implementation successfully. The self imposed target of 80% was already exceeded by half the year after the starting of circulation transactions through the self-service station. In the second year the average usage of 93% was 13% higher than the target originally set. Within the first year of implementation the staff reductions in the circulation section met the required efficiency saving. He suggested that the worth examining aspect would be to study the processes involved in other libraries to establish the common themes and to assess if the Pilkington library's experience with RFID was an anomaly.

Feng[93] in 2010 in his paper entitled "Research for application of RFID in library" emphasized on the advantages that RFID technology had such as rapid scanning, contactless reading, long life, high information content, etc. He felt that RFID technology can be used to manage location of library collections; their circulation; book classification; standard codes; data collection, etc. thereby it can improve the efficiency of the library. He concluded that as a new and still developing technology, RFID is in its emerging stage and there are many difficulties and problems in its use such as its standard are not defined, it is costly, has security issues and problems in integration with the library management system and so on, but it has great potential for development. RFID technology is the future of libraries and in Chinese libraries it will achieve good results.

In the same year Ustundag and Kilinc[94] in their article "Design and development of RFID based library information system" stated that RFID technology has found wide application in many sectors such as automotive, retail, healthcare, logistics and libraries. They described an RFID based Library Information System (RLIS) for a Turkish library. They examined the long term benefits of RLIS and opined that RFID can benefit the libraries in processing, book tracking and security of library collection. The existing barcode systems can be enhanced by RFID as this technology provides additional features such as self checkout and return and also has the added feature of security against theft. They thought that RFID will reduce loss of library items and save time spent in searching for books incorrectly shelved. Stock-taking can easily be done by simply walking along a stack as the RFID tags on the books can be read while they are still on the shelves. They concluded that librarians have always been seeking new technology to improve their services and management and the RFID technology offers potentially a lot more than the barcode.

Zhu et al.[95] in 2010 in their paper "Design of an intelligent book conveyor based on RFID" described that the RFID Intelligent Book Conveyor used microprocessors embedded in them instead of the traditional computer and the conveyors are portable. They were of the opinion that due to user friendly interface and simple operation of conveyors the librarian is freed from the repetitive work of book sorting and shelving thus greatly improving their work efficiency. They concluded that the solution to the two main problems which are related to libraries provided by conveyors are: firstly the library can only rely on manual book shelf searching which is time-consuming and inefficient and second is that OPAC searching can't help the reader to find the book on the corresponding shelf. It has such features as accurate positioning to enable easy finding, real- time updating of the database and navigation function in the OPAC that encourages the reader to use OPAC inquiry terminal and thus greatly enhances the service level.

During the period 2005-2010 many libraries had started experimenting with the use of RFID technology in their libraries. The technology was mostly being used in the areas of circulation and stock taking. The users had started getting familiar with the technology and were becoming aware of its benefits in terms of accuracy and time saving capacity. However, the main hindrances were the cost of the technology, privacy issues and lack of standards.

3.1.3. 2011- 2018

In 2011 Abdullah et al[96] in their article entitled "Library shelf management system using RFID technology" stated that the task of Graphical User Interface (GUI) is to store detailed information of the books to the database, create a Shelf ID that can be coded on the RFID tag. The system uses this code to find the books on the selected shelf. If the data equals to the selected shelf number, it means that the book is in correct position but if the data does not equal to the selected shelf number, there is a beep that alerts the librarian that the book is misplaced. The information of a book is stored in the database and on the tag and the interface between the RFID system and the tag successfully accomplishes this application. They opined that library shelf management system assisted the librarians in more efficient shelf management and in finding any mis-shelved books thus reducing the human intervention. They concluded that further studies need to be done in the area of ascertaining the performance of the system in terms of the accuracy of the reading process since the system involved sending and receiving signals and data in a specific interval of time.

Mehrjerdi[97] in 2011 in her paper “RFID: the big player in the libraries of the future” emphasised the key areas related to the future libraries having RFID-based system which included initial cost involved, cost of IT infrastructure, RFID skilled man power, data security, patron privacy, etc. She also enumerated some of the key benefits of RFID in libraries like stock management, efficient circulation, better inventory control, data accuracy and reliability, prevention of theft, etc. She said that RFID system can be integrated into existing library system so as to improve the efficiency of the main functions of any library such as stocktaking, book searching and quality of services being provided. She concluded that the future library is going to be very different from today’s library that will partly be made possible with the aid of technologies like RFID.

Repanovici and Cristea[98] in 2011 in their article “RFID technology used in small library - case study at Transilvania University” proposed open source library management system Koha with RFID technology as an economical solution with wide applicability. They opined that Koha is suitable for automation and computerization of both big and small libraries and can be implemented in libraries based on bar codes or RFID technology. They discussed the various problems encountered during the implementation of RFID technology in libraries. They are: patron privacy; inter-library services due to differences in tags used or software; metal shelves influencing readers and sensors; RFID technologies being more expensive than barcodes and security strips. They concluded that a library of the 21st century requires an automated system to modernize the activities within a library system for identifying, inventorying and managing books, magazines, CDs, tapes, videos and etc. Due to the limitations of the barcodes and security strips (Electronic Article Surveillance or EAS), only RFID technology can achieve this.

Walsh[99] in 2011 in his paper "Blurring the boundaries between our physical and electronic libraries: Location-aware technologies, QR codes and RFID tags" considered the use of such technologies as QR codes, GPS and RFID to personalize the learning experience in academic libraries. He reported the use of QR codes at the University of Huddersfield. He found that the location-aware technologies being used in most of the libraries were impractical. The use QR codes have significant barriers and it was preferable to use RFID tags that already were being widely used for other purposes, to create smarter libraries. Libraries had increasingly started using RFID tags for their stocks and occasionally for library or campus smart cards as well. He outlined the additional benefits which should be considered that offset the cost of RFID tags in libraries i.e. by using them to personalize their learning experineces. He concluded that while most of the technologies have been used in experimental way in libraries, none had yet used RFID tags for any other purpose than stock circulation and control.

Zimerman[100] in 2011 in his paper "Radio Frequency Identification (RFID): time to take another look" revealed that prices of RFID tags and equipment had reduced significantly. He was of the opinion that once the RFID technology is set up, it will give the task of circulation and collection management to the computer rather than burden the staff. Collection management is of the utmost importance to any modern library and that can be favourably performed with efficiency by the RFID system. He was of the opinions that if a library cannot afford it in one go it should consider implementing it in phases. He concluded that since costs of the RFID components are coming down the libraries can improve their systems enormously by using it to increase their efficiency. He opined that any library that has the budget should seriously consider implementing it.

Gibb et al[101] in their paper entitled "The application of RFIDs in libraries: an assessment of technological, management and professional issues" provided an overview of the RFID technology with reference to the library functions and raised the ethical concerns for the library profession. The technologies involved in RFID and issues raised by its general application were reviewed by them. They gave a general view of library activities and identified the potential application areas within the library sector based on it. They were of the opinion that ethically librarians have to protect the interests of their patrons as far as practicable and they have to maintain confidentiality with respect to the data concerning their transactions with the library. They suggested that the library professional should extend the training and education of users and employees to ensure that there is a shared understanding of the role of RFID that it is committed to delivering benefits to the users. They concluded that "does this work?" attitude should not be allowed to over-rule the ethical one as the library profession has always maintained a noble tradition of freedom of thought and freedom of access.

In 2011 Thornley et al[102] in their paper "Do RFIDs (radio frequency identifier devices) provide new ethical dilemmas for librarians and information professionals?" said that there is increased risk of surveillance with use of RFID which raises privacy concerns in the library environment. They analysed such issues as a series of ethical dilemmas which the librarian has to face with regard to information, library patrons and the social environment or politics of a state. They opined that to provide information from an object to a user using the RFID technology one needs to have an access to the Library Management System. They concluded that the new tools for data collection using RFID technology, the privacy of library user can be broken and it will certainly raise new ethical issues for the library and information professionals. They suggested that the librarians needed to have an ethical policy framework so that these new anticipated challenges can be dealt with efficiently.

In 2012 Ayre[103] in his article entitled "Library RFID systems for identification, security, and materials handling" stated that RFID-based self-check is more convenient for the users because they do not have to identify the barcode and align the item properly in line of sight with the scanner. He quoted a library RFID survey conducted in 2012 where 98 percent of libraries had implemented RFID and were making use of Self-Check system for self-service. He discussed some security concerns related to RFID and stated that the in the study of RFID versus EM effective security is roughly equal and neither of them is perfect. He opined that RFID security issues should be addressed if a library is implementing an RFID system. However, primary justification for switching from a barcode/EM system to RFID shouldn't be only to better the library's security.

In the same year Sun and Chen[104] in their paper "A proposed model for library stacks management" stated that the space in a library has again become a primary issue faced by librarians in recent times and they presented a new model for stack management in libraries.

They developed a new stacks management model called "parent–child–grandchild model" by employing the RFID as well as the management principles that involved changing the layout of the book stacks. In this a model, the book stacks are arranged into three sections, one large ("parent"), one medium ("child") and one small ("grandchild"). The entire printed collection of a library has to be comprised of three sections, based upon different functions and use of the stacks. They opined that a library must have a good RFID support facility which would assist the library staff to effectively manage the printed collection and facilitate library users in finding the physical location of books. They have further discussed the various processes facilitated with RFID such as transaction, production, governance, interaction etc. They concluded that the new model once implemented will revolutionize the library scene by achieving not only better stack management but also present an attractive and friendlier image of the library.

In 2013 Dwivedi et al[105] in their paper "RFID systems in libraries: an empirical examination of factors affecting system use and user satisfaction" stated that many library operations and management are repetitive in nature and require performing activities that are painstaking, time consuming and labour -intensive. To eliminate this and in order to increase efficiency and effectiveness, many libraries are shifting over to automation of majority of their activities by deploying RFID technology instead of the barcode systems. However, they have highlighted some concerns related to the implementation of RFID technology that include the cost, error in reading ultra-high-frequency tags near a human body, multi item readings, etc. They found that RFID-related studies largely concentrate on organizational, technical and implementation aspects, and less attention has been paid to understanding its utility and user-satisfaction aspects. They developed a conceptual model to examine factors that affect the use and user satisfaction of RFID-based systems. They found from their study that factors that have a significant positive influence on system use and users' satisfaction such as system quality, information quality, service quality, etc. are important. They said that the users prefer using the RFID stations (self-check out/self check-in) for the issue / return of books from the library.

Makori[106] in 2013 in her paper entitled "Adoption of Radio Frequency Identification technology in university libraries: a Kenyan perspective" studied the adoption of RFID technology in university libraries of Kenya for handling and supporting information service activities. She outlined the various problems that were hindering the adoption of the RFID technology in universities of Kenya. The various reasons were the lack of policy for information communication, business approach lacking, market opportunities being limited, negotiation skills lacking, lack of funds and ICT competencies and skills. She suggested that library information professionals and ICT professionals must put in unrelenting efforts to implement RFID technology and ensure its proper usage so that information work, services and activities in university libraries can be properly built, strengthened, improved and supported. She was of the opinion that information professionals in university libraries must be empowered with appropriate ICT knowledge and skills that are necessary in the modern information environment.

In 2013 Sugie[107] in his research paper "Application of Radio Frequency Identification technology to study library users' information-seeking behavior" analysed the approaches of information-seeking behaviour in the university library in Saitama, Japan to assess RFID technology. Three undergraduate students participated in this experiment and were given 40 minutes to complete the tasks. Data on "travelling paths of participants," "time to explore each zone," "time to explore primary and secondary sources," "time to explore information sources by subject," and "modified tag records" gave information regarding the search patterns of users. He was of the opinion that RFID technology effectively revealed and analyzed the information-seeking behaviour pattern of library users. It can be used to assess if the services or location of resources in a particular library are appropriate. The biggest advantage of the technology was that more data could be easily and accurately collected than was possible using the traditional methods. However, he also noted the disadvantages of the RFID were that much effort was required in locating the appropriate place for tags on items and also that the RFID system could not guarantee enough read range accuracy. He found that the proposed method ensured sufficiently accurate data to analyze and illustrate library users' information-seeking behaviour. It provides much more accurate data than the traditional research methods and that too with least effort.

Zhang[108] in the same year in his article "Study on intelligent library system based on RFID technology" studied the pros and cons of the library management system based on RFID. He has detailed the concept, components and principles of working of the RFID and explored its application and potential uses in the libraries all over the world. He stated that in the last almost 10 years the RFID technology has been adopted in the libraries world over and more than 2,000 libraries were using RFID in 2013 and its adoption is increasing at the rate of 30% annually. He was of the opinion that the adoption of RFID technology in libraries is costly and the project is long-term with a high-impact. The decision-making for the library is complex and has to be based on the analysis of feasibility. He suggested that the library management before taking a decision should comprehensively analyze the existing industry scenario, business processes and management methods. Appropriate strategy needs to be developed from the point of view of economy, technology and security. The advantages and problems need to be analyzed and then make a secure, flexible, humanized and intelligent library decision.

He laid emphasis on the advantages of using RFID in the library system that include having simple and quick self-service, efficiency improvement of the librarian, saving manpower required in the library, and to provide a secure environment for users. He also examined the constraints related to RFID in the university libraries like technical standards, cost, system integration, security, etc.

In 2014, Guo, Huang & Chen[109], Huang &Chen studied the UHF-RFID data model construction scheme for university libraries. They further explained and defined six user data elements different from ISO28560: version, owner library identifiers, temporary item location, subject, International Standard Serial Number (ISSN) and International Standard Book Number (ISBN). They are in the view that this standard will offer uniform data models for university libraries to comply with, integrate the disordered market and further make the opening, unified, compatible and interoperable RFID application possible.

In 2015, Fujisaki[110], stated that because the RFID system enables non-contact communication, various services and applications including the management of a library catalogue are possible. However, author is in the view that the system is affected easily by neighboring environment and the resonant frequency, thus the communication performance is degraded.

Timoshenko[111], in 2016 studies the application of the RFID in Russian libraries. In Russia, the first experimental RFID project was implemented in 2006 at the Russian Public Scientific Technical Library (RPSTL). He studied stages of the emergence and development of the RFID at Russian libraries and analyzes the current state of library RFID systems. The study founded that RFID has significantly improved the efficiency of working with paper documents, thus helping the harmonic integration of the traditional technologies for working with library-fund documents into the modern concepts of the existence of libraries.

In 2018, Sammeta & Madara[112] in their research work given the outline of contributions of RFID innovation, and its utilization in Amity University, Dubai Campus. They recommended that variables like framework quality, utilization and client fulfillment emphatically impact consumer's states of mind towards RFID-empowered services.

After 2010 there was a rapid increase in the number of libraries that had adopted the RFID technology. Not only that it was a convenient and easy to use technology it was also increasing the efficiency and quality of services being provided by the libraries. Most of the authorities in academic institutions were realizing this and were ready to provide funds for the same. This gave a boost to the already popular technology with the library professionals due to its benefits, convenience and accuracy and the RFID technology was rapidly adopted worldwide.

3.2. RFID USE IN LIBRARIES IN INDIA

Not much literature has been published in India about the RFID technology. However, some significant studies in the context of India are given below:

In 2005 Shahid[113] in his article described the RFID technology and its components. He highlighted the key features of RFID technology in libraries like self-charging/ discharging, reliability, high-speed inventorying, etc. He suggested that if best practices and guidelines are followed religiously the use of RFID technology in libraries does not pose a threat. He opined that the use of RFID in a library increases the speed of borrowing a book and check inventories, so that the staff is freed from routine work to perform more user-centric tasks. He concluded that RFID system is a comprehensive system that addresses both the security issues and material tracking requirement of a library, it saves money and return on the investment is visible quickly.

Narayanan et al[114] in 2005 in their paper "Implementing RFID in library: methodologies, advantages and disadvantages" discussed the RFID technology, its components, implementation methodologies in library and advantages and disadvantages in library. They opined that the adoption of the technology in Indian libraries is comparatively recent and thus many features of the technology are still not understood very well. Although the unique benefits and flexibility of RFID is well recognised, the technology is not yet widely understood or being used in the library environment. The cost involved and the return on investment were not clear. They concluded in their study that RFID was increasing in popularity amongst Indian libraries, and the libraries that were early adopters of this technology felt that it makes economic sense, for large as well as small libraries.

In 2006 Naga Lakshmi et al[115] in their paper "A security mechanism for library management system using low cost RFID tags" proposed a library management system using low cost RFID tags as a secure measure for a book or a magazine or a CD that is identified with the RFID tag. When a book needs to be issued to a user of the library, the RFID reader reads the information of that book stored on its RFID tag and compares it with the information of the book in the Online Public Access Catalogue (OPAC). The book is issued to the user after verifying his identity according to the information already stored in the database. No unauthorized person or a person not a member of the library can get a book issued as the RFID reader immediately responds and makes sure that the book is not issued. If someone tries to remove or temper with the RFID tag, it can be traced by using the location device. They found that RFID components are used in libraries for various purposes such as identification of books, self checkout and check in, theft control, inventory taking and also for sorting and conveying of library books and audio visual material in some libraries. With these applications libraries can have significant savings in labor costs, enhance service to the users, reduce book thefts and they can provide a constantly updated record of their collections. They concluded that with the new generation of RFID chips with ISO standard 15693 now available in the market the libraries using this technology are not dependent on the vendor for their lifeline.

In the same year Selamat and Majlis[116] in their study "Challenges in implementing RFID tag in a conventional library" discussed the implementation of RFID technology in IMEN University in Malaysia. They stated that to improve the management of assets of any library RFID technology is the best alternative technology available in the market recently. Instead of the bar codes and magnetic strips the RFID tags were now were now being used to perform the function of identification of items and prevention of theft. They opined that for implementing the RFID technology, some of the difficulties faced were related to integration of the system, operating the new system alongside the existing system, and the procedural changes involved. One of the main challenges faced by libraries was how to integrate RFID tags with the existing Library Management System. They were of the opinion that with the self-check counter the process of borrowing and returning of books becomes automatic and involve the library professionals to a lesser extent; therefore the librarian is able to focus on providing more effective service to the library patrons. They further suggested that while the conversion process to the new technology is in progress, it is necessary to have the previous system, for example barcode, running parallel to RFID so that the library functions can be performed normally.

Kumar et al[117] in the year 2007 in their paper

"Development of RFID interface for LMS: Solutions and techniques" examined the various issues with regard to the integration of Library Management Software (LMS) with the RFID technology. They conducted an experiment in Information and Library Network (INFLIBNET), India on the development of an interface with the library management software SOUL being used by INLIBNET, based on SIP2 (Standard Interchange Protocol version 2), which is the accepted standard for RFID implementation in libraries. They were of the opinion that the SIP2 interface developed for integrating RFID with SOUL is a general solution that can be adopted with slight modifications for integration of any other LMS software. Introduction of such a solution in the academic libraries in the country will speed up the automation process to make the library a fully user-centric automated library.

In the same year Ghosh[118] in his paper "Application of RFID technology in Sardar Vallabhbhai National Institute of Technology (SVNIT), Surat" said that the latest and most advanced technology employed in different industries for security and theft detection is the RFID technology. He pointed out that the RFID system is most accurate, cost effective and requires less manpower to handle a library, although it is initially costly to implement and has some demerits. He recommended that if the budget of an institution does not permit the library to implement the complete system in one go, it may be implemented in phases. Finally, he highlighted that the 21st century librarians should go ahead with this advanced technology and not compromise.

Again in 2007 Pattanaik and Pattnaik[119] in their article "RFID: the security for library" highlighted the origin and presented an overview of the technology associated with implementation of RFID in libraries. They have discussed the main standards and components of the RFID system. They were of the opinion today only a few libraries are employing this technology, but as it has customizable features and is being improved upon continuously, the libraries have started to get involved in its development. They have discussed the major concerns that need to be addressed before implementing this technology like the barriers of technology, culture, finance, lack of proper standards, blocking of the RF wave, etc.

In 2008 Singh and Midha[120] in their article "RFID: a new technology in library management systems" have discussed the use of RFID technology in libraries and have stressed on its various benefits like high speed circulation operations with self-charging/discharging, its high reliability, high-speed inventory taking, handling of materials is automated, extended life of RFID tags, etc. They have also noted the disadvantages of RFID system such as its high cost, possibility of removal of exposed tags, etc. They have specified the features to be taken into consideration while evaluating the RFID vendors that include the security aspect, reader collision, capacity of tag memory, anti-collision standards, etc. They summed up that popularity of RFID technology is increasing among libraries, as the early adopters of this technology have proved that it makes good economic sense libraries both large and small.

Galhotra and Galhotra[121] in 2009 in their article entitled "Application of Radio Frequency Identification Technology in libraries" discussed the extent to which this technology has been introduced in the Indian libraries and its various advantages and disadvantages of using RFID. They compared RFID technology with barcodes and suggested that RFID has an advantage over barcode. They discussed various RFID standards and concluded that though RFID is costlier in comparison with the barcodes technology, it has proved its worth for automated data collection and identification applications. They opined that if some standards for uniformity are formulated so as RFID equipment from different manufactures can be used interchangeably, its market will grow exponentially.

In the year 2009 Bansode and Desale[122] did a case study on "Implementation of RFID technology in University of Pune Library" provided an overview of implementation of the RFID project, problems faced and benefits realised after the implementation of the technology. They enumerated the problems being faced by library staff such as the technology experts not being available, unwillingness of the users towards the change over, standards of RFID not being available, etc. The reported major advantages of implementing RFID, by them, were in the areas of stock inventory taking, tracking of books on the shelves and those missing, speedy check-in and check-out of books, etc. In conclusion they said that RFID technology, inspite of the various difficulties in its implementation, gives a fillip to the library services, as less manpower is required to service more books and users.

In the same year Vasishta[123] in her paper "Roadmap for RFID implementation in Central Library, PEC University of Technology" described the basic and optional components required for RFID technology to be working smoothly. She has discussed various problems faced and their possible solutions during the process of implementation of RFID applications. She concluded that though the RFID technology is costly for many libraries to opt, but it has proved its worth by yielding good results for libraries that have adopted it worldwide. It has well demonstrated the ability to make management process of the library more convenient. The synthesis of the latest technology like RFID with libraries has created wonders and resulted in the empowerment of both the library management as well as the users.

In 2010, Margam[124] in his paper "RFID technology implementation in two libraries in New Delhi" has studied the implementation and use of RFID technology in the libraries of two institutions: Indian Law Institute (New Delhi) and National Social Science Documentation Centre,

(New Delhi). He reported that after the implementation of RFID technology in the libraries of both the institutes, the check-in and check-out time of library materials was reduced. The time required was found to be less than 20 seconds per item. The usage of the libraries was also reported to have increased. The most significant challenge faced for the implementation of RFID technology was its high cost. However, keeping in view the manifold advantages of RFID technology for libraries he recommended the use of the technology for other libraries also so as to provide faster and more efficient services to their patrons. He has suggested that as the cost factor involved to implement RFID technology is very high, it is not possible to change the technology frequently. Thus only good quality tags should be used. He also suggested that anti-virus protection should be provided for RFID technology. He reached the conclusion that the libraries of future will all have RFID technology. It is expected that with its wider use, soon the cost of the technology will reduce and more and more libraries in India will be able to adopt this technology.

In the year 2011 Radha[125] in her paper "Deployment of RFID (Radio Frequency Identification) at Indian academic libraries: issues and best practice" identified the areas and activities that the RFID technology is applicable to in libraries like self check in/checkout of library items without the help of the library staff, anti-theft security, stock management, etc. It comprises of many components such as the RFID tags, staff station, security gate, self service units, shelf assistant, etc. and there are many more areas its application can be extended to in future. She concluded that RFID implementation involves many issues and has many advantages. Most of the Indian institutions have started adopting RFID for keeping track of the library materials, for detecting thefts and automated check in /out service, etc.

In the year 2012 Pandey et al.[126] in their paper

"Application of RFID technology in libraries and role of librarian" have given the advantages of adopting RFID technology in libraries that includes self check-out and check-in, accuracy of the technology, convenient inventory management, longevity of the life of RFID tag, faster circulation of library material, enhanced security, etc. They however, said that librarians have to take steps to ensure the privacy of their patrons. In conclusion they have stated that RFID technology being more effective, convenient and cost effective, has slowly started replacing the old and traditional bar-code and electromagnetic security strips technology.

In 2015, Prasanna & Megalan[127] in their study conducted a survey of Library automation system using RFID. He opined that the management of the book is very complicated and time consuming process. In his study he found that students generally altered the location of the books in the library. In the proposed work, physical location of the library books can be found quickly using RFID. It reduces the searching time and hence the unnecessary wastage of time is avoided.

In 2017, Singh & Mahajan[128], conducted a study on application of RFID in libraries and information centre in Indian Libraries. They investigated the present status of RFID application, benefits realised after implementing RFID, problems faced during RFID adoption and its implementation in the libraries and information centres of Northern India. The study observed that all the selected libraries in Northern India are in the initial stages of RFID implementation and they are realizing the benefits of its implementation which include reduction in queue at circulation desk/counter, extended hours of circulation without additional staff, library collection has become more secure, etc. At the same time, library staffs facing some problems with the use of RFID technology.

3.3. CONCLUSION

The study of the literature on application of RFID technology in libraries worldwide reveals that before 2001 no significant application of the technology in libraries was there. RFID technology was being used in other sectors including mining, aviation, logistics, etc. and was adopted in libraries only after 2000. In the Indian scenario such studies were conducted only after another 5 years. The above review of literature reveals that most of the studies on the RFID technology in academic libraries have mainly been carried out on the theoretical aspects including the advantages/disadvantages and problems related to RFID application. However, not many empirical studies are available to show the actual usage of RFID technology in libraries either in India or abroad.

The main concerns in adopting the RFID technology in libraries were the cost factor, Return on Investment, compatibility with the Library Management Software, lack of uniform standards for libraries and security issues of the library users' data. But slowly the library authorities realized that the advantages of adopting the technology outnumber the doubts. After suitably modifying the technology to the requirements of libraries the technology has been adopted by many large libraries abroad and also in India. Now many smaller libraries that could not afford the cost in one go are adopting the technology in phased manner and according to their needs. These studies show that the RFID technology is definitely advantageous for libraries and is here to stay.

4
RFID in Libraries : Lessons Learnt

Due to the low cost of the barcode technology, most of the libraries around the world are using it for circulation management. However, the main constraints related to barcode technology are: it always requires a line-of-sight, does not provide security of library collection, does not offer any benefit for collection management and is becoming very difficult for the libraries to satisfy the increasing demands of the users. Thus comes up the need to implement a new technology to improve the library circulation management, inventory and security of library collections.

Librarians are always known as early adopters of technology and they have started using RFID to provide circulation services in a more effective and efficient manner, for security of library collections and to satisfy the increasing demands of the users. The use of RFID by libraries over the last few years has grown dramatically. A large number of libraries in developed countries have adopted this technology. Observing the usefulness and efficiency of RFID, libraries in the developing countries like India have also started implementing RFID in libraries. As a small number of libraries in India have introduced RFID, it is high time to study the application of RFID technology in libraries, keeping in view its problems and benefits.

This study seeks to provide a method to help libraries to evaluate whether the RFID is feasible in their libraries in its present situation. The study will look at the state of implementation of RFID in the libraries of Northern India and use the data gathered there from to provide suggestions and indications of the costs and benefits that other libraries might expect. There cannot be one single formula for determining the standard costs and benefits that can be obtained with implementing RFID technology that would be applicable to every library since each library is different, with variation in goals, differences in collections, their size, staff, labour costs, open hours and ways of providing service. To provide a general evaluative method and pointing out which of a variety of factors need to be considered in determining the value of the technology to the institution, is the aim of this study.

The main objective of the library is to provide quality services to its users and evaluate these services continuously for their improvements. In this regard, the task of this study is to ascertain the purpose, present status, benefits realized and problems faced with the implementation of RFID technology. The results of the present study will give some valuable suggestions/ recommendations to the librarians who have already implemented RFID technology in terms of its better utilisation and at the same time it will help those librarians who want to implement RFID system in their libraries.

The basic purpose of implementing RFID is to provide better and efficient library services such as self checkout/check-in of library materials, security of library books and efficient tracking of library materials throughout the library. It is necessary to study the purpose, the benefits realized after implementing RFID and various problems being faced by library staff in implementing such technology. It is also necessary to know the perception of users and staff from time to time, so that necessary measures can be initiated for better utilization. Since the libraries and information centers in the Northern India are unexplored for such a study the present study is very timely and fruitful to examine the application of RFID technology in libraries and information centers in this region.

4.1. METHODOLOGY

In social science research, the questionnaire method is widely used for data collection. In the present study also, questionnaire and survey methods were employed for eliciting the needed information. The questionnaires were pre-tested and modifications were incorporated based on the pre-test experience. The final questionnaires were used for data collection. Two well designed structured questionnaires covering the relevant aspects of the study were used to collect the data. The comprehensive "Questionnaires" were prepared, one for librarians/ concerned library professionals and another for users to collect the data required for the present study. The first one was to collect the information regarding the purpose and key factors for implementing RFID, problems faced during the process and benefits realised after implementing RFID in libraries.

The second questionnaire was to know the users' perception and their satisfaction level with the use of RFID technology. The questionnaires were personally distributed among the users in the libraries under investigation. Every possible effort was made to obtain the data from different categories of users. Interview and observation method were also adopted wherever required to make data and information more authentic. Four categories of users i.e. faculty members, research scholars, post graduate students and under graduate students have been covered. Data thus obtained was entered into MS Excel and analyzed using SPSS 16.0 v software.

This study is first of its kind in India and a similar study was conducted in USA by Engel, Elena (2006)[129] RFID Implementations in 27 California Libraries: Costs and Benefits. The objectives of both the studies are almost similar in aspects of purpose; planning and implementation; benefits realized; problems faced and satisfaction level etc. thus the data presented in this chapter is on the pattern of the Engel study.

LIMITATIONS OF THE STUDY

Due to certain limitations, it was not possible to cover all libraries and information centres of Northern India that have implemented RFID. Hence, the present study is limited to the Central, State and Deemed universities recognised by the UGC and IITs situated in Northern region of India which have implemented RFID in their libraries and the study was conducted in the year 2014 for doctoral research. Due to the small data size, the variation in the systems and the way they were implemented, it is difficult to draw conclusions that can be generalized to all libraries. However, the responses collected from libraries can provide indications about costs and benefits that may be possible for other libraries to derive from RFID. The data set will become more widely significant as more libraries over the years adopt RFID systems. The libraries though will also need to collect RFID "before and after" data that can help illustrate what magnitude of changes can be expected after implementation. Thus, the future studies would be able to draw more general conclusions.

4.1. Libraries Included

The present study covers nine academic institutions

of Northern India spanning central, state and deemed universities as well as IITs of Northern India. They are the Gautam Buddha University (Greater Noida); Indian Institute of Technology (Roorkee); Indian Institute of Technology (Delhi); Indian Law Institute (New Delhi); Panjab University (Chandigarh); Punjabi University (Patiala); Ram Manohar Lohiya Law University (Lucknow); University of Jammu (Jammu) and University of Kashmir (Srinagar).

Of the 9 selected libraries that responded to the initial survey, 7 were university libraries and two were libraries of IITs. Two libraries had collections smaller than 50,000; two had collections between 150,000 and 200,000 items; and five had collections between 300,000 and 400,000.

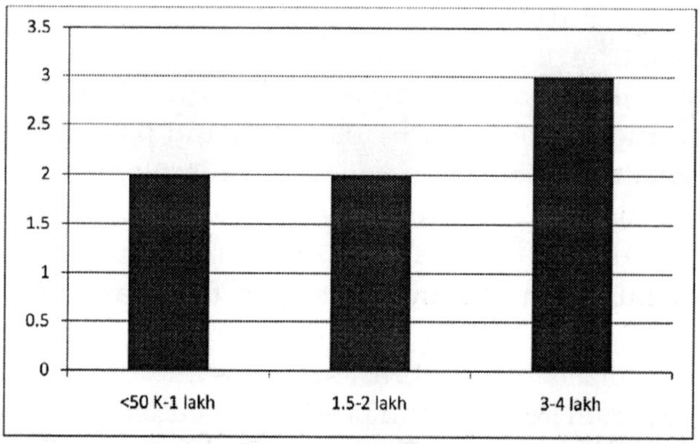

Fig. 4.1. Libraries by Size of Collection Tagged

4.2. INITIATION OF RFID PROJECT

The analysis reveals that five libraries (i.e., 55.5%) started using RFID within the same year the project was initiated, while remaining four libraries (i.e., 44.4%) took about 12-18 months to start the RFID facility in their libraries.

A comprehensive overview of all the selected institutions of Northern India indicates that all the libraries in Northern India selected under the study are fully automated and functional with the RFID system for automated issue/return of the documents. The first library that had initiated the RFID project is University of Jammu (Jammu) which initiated it in 2004, followed by Indian Law Institute (New Delhi) which initiated the project in 2006. The remaining libraries initiated this project during the period 2008 to 2010.

It also shows that all the selected libraries in Northern India have RFID components (i.e., Self-check-in/Check-out, Book Drop, Shelf Management Reader/ Digital Library Assistant, Staff Workstations/Programming Stations, security gates, etc.) in their respective libraries. Out of the above nine institutions in Northern India except three libraries i.e. Ram Manohar Lohiya Law University (Lucknow); University of Jammu (Jammu) and Indian Law Institute (New Delhi) the remaining institutions have fully implemented RFID technology and are using Self-check-out/check-in/ Book drop system which allows users to do self-issue and return of the documents without going to the circulation counter.

4.3. GOALS: WHY THE LIBRARIES CHOSE RFID?

The primary and secondary goals for implementing RFID were asked from participating libraries. They were also told to indicate if there were goals on our list that specifically were not goals for their implementation. The list of goals on our survey is shown in the figure below:

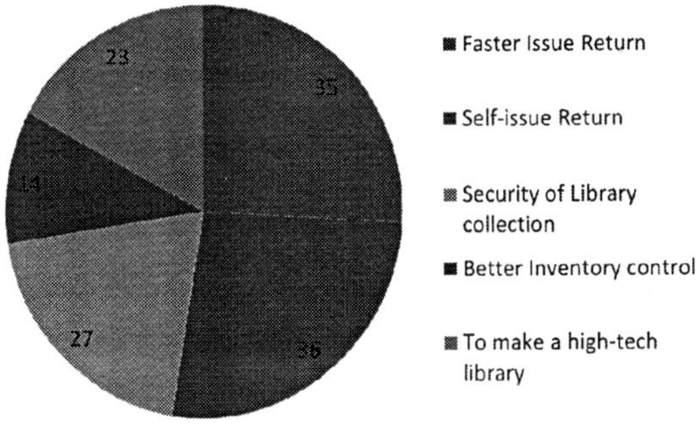

Fig. 4.2. Goals of implementing RFID

Libraries in our survey were greatly interested in introducing or increasing the rate of patron self-check and in the faster issue return so as to reduce lines at the circulation desk. After those, the libraries were interested in security capabilities of the RFID systems. The least preferred purpose for implementing RFID technology was "better inventory control". This may be due to the fact that out of the nine selected libraries, only six libraries (i.e., 66.7%) have Digital Library Assistant/Shelf Management Reader. It was also observed during the personal visit to the participating libraries that all the libraries are in the initial stage of RFID implementation and their main focus is to run the Self-check-in /check-out system smoothly. After a certain period of time (i.e., 3-5) years, they might consider using Digital Library Assistant for inventory control in their respective libraries.

During the discussions with the library professionals in some of the libraries it was reported that staff crunch is also one of the main purposes for implementing the RFID technology. It was difficult for them to depute any professional staff at circulation desk. Hence, they were looking for a technology which could replace staff at the circulation desk and with the implementation of RFID technology, all the work of issue/ return of the books is now being performed using the RFID system. They have deputed a non professional staff at the circulation counter who assists the users if they face any problem while using the RFID system.

4.4. KEY FACTORS FOR RFID ADOPTION

The selected libraries were studied in order to determine the key factors affecting the implementation of the RFID technology in the libraries.

The most significant factor for RFID adoption in the selected libraries in Northern India was the top management support (55%) in terms of financial, technical, infrastructural, institutional and administrative support, etc. Many libraries perceived RFID benefits (33%) i.e., self-issue/return, security of library collections, inventory control, etc. for adoption of RFID technology. Surprisingly the least important key factor for RFID adoption in libraries was the "user demand". The significant difference noticed in the reasons for adopting RFID technology by IIT libraries and university libraries was that the IITs had full top management support followed by perceived RFID benefits rather than the university libraries.

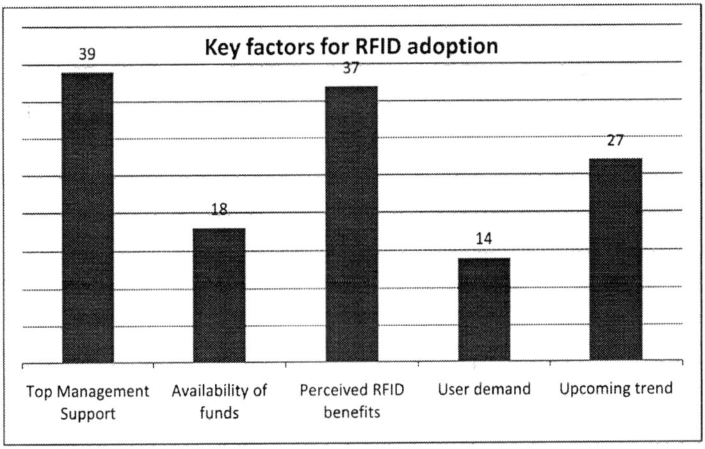

Fig. 4.3. Key factor for RFID adoption

During the study it was ascertained that the main purpose for implementing RFID technology in the libraries was self- issue/return so that the users can issue/return books themselves without any assistance from the library staff. The need to circulate more books with less staff was a factor for many of the libraries in our survey as faster issue/return of books was possible through RFID assisted circulation desk. Some libraries that had already adopted the new or renovated facility reported a great increase in circulation. This technology has made it possible for libraries to replace staff at the circulation desk as all the work of issue/return of the books is now being performed using the RFID system.

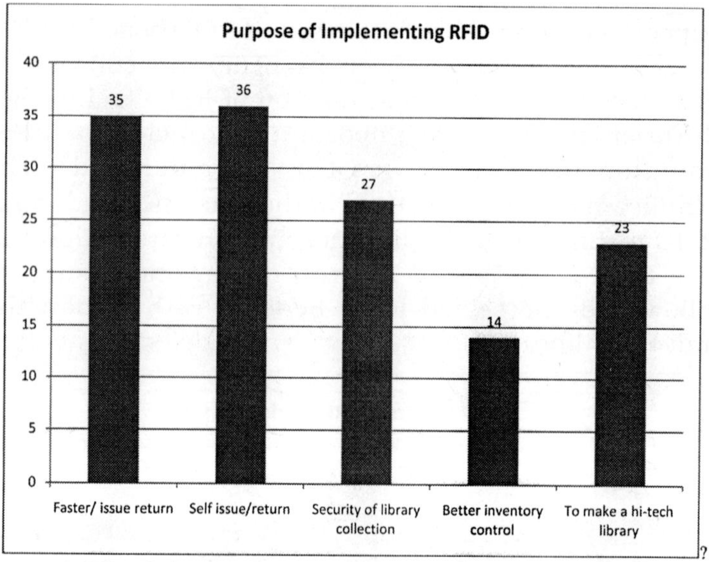

Fig. 4.4. Key purpose of implementing RFID

As frequently as circulation goals the security capabilities of RFID were mentioned as either a primary or secondary goal. The least preferred purpose for implementing RFID technology was better inventory control. This may be due to the fact that out of the selected libraries, only 66.7% libraries have Digital Library Assistant/Shelf Management Reader.

4.5. RFID PLANNING AND IMPLEMENTATION

The data collected shows that in the selected libraries the RFID project was initiated earliest in the year 2004 and was fully functional by the year 2011. It is clear that 55.5% libraries started using RFID within the same year the project was initiated, while remaining 44.4% libraries took about 12-18 months to start the RFID facility in their libraries. Some of the crucial factors for successful planning and implementation of a new technology are the funds to be provided by the institution; proper financial and administrative steps to be followed for its execution; coordination between the vendor and staff and post installation support and training of the staff.

4.5.1. Funds

The funding for RFID project is the key to implement the technology in the library. The source of funding for RFID project, total budget for RFID project, provision of recurring budget for AMC and purchase of new RFID tags are the important financial issues. It was found that 77.8% of selected libraries under study received special grant for RFID project from their parent institution, whereas 22.2% spent funds out of regular library budget for this project. However, it was revealed that no grant was either provided by the state or central government for the RFID project. It was further revealed that 66.7% libraries under study do have a recurring budget provision of Rs. 1 lakh to 2.5 lakh for AMC, purchase of tags, etc.

During discussions with the librarians which do not have recurring budget provision, it was observed they initially purchased a certain number of tags and have tagged only that collection which is in circulation excluding reference sources, theses and dissertations, periodicals, CD/DVD, etc. As far as AMC is concerned, it has been given free initially for three years by the vendor. After the expiry of the free term of AMC they would seek budget from the authorities.

4.5.2. Planning and Execution

The implementation of RFID project involves proper planning and execution of the project. It involves various activities like preparing a tender document, tender specifications, selection of companies that apply against the tender, negotiation with the vendors, etc. Different persons who belong to administration, finance, IT, library staff, etc. are required to execute the project. Most of the libraries i.e. 88.9% under study confirmed having special committee formed for the purpose with experts from within the institution as well as some had members from other institutions also that had already implemented RFID in their institutions. The committees had representatives of administrative bodies such as the Dean University Instructions, Director, Deputy Director, Deans, etc. 55.5% libraries reported to having had RFID experts from other institutions in their RFID implementation committees. In all the institutions, the committees had the librarian, IT experts and accounts and finance personnel as members.

4.5.3. Implementation

The implementation process involved various steps such as arranging presentations; visiting other institutions that already have installed RFID technology and are using it; floating tender for fair selection of the vendor; doing a pilot project to test the feasibility of the technology; and finally the training of the staff not only to familiarize them with the technology but also get the best output from it. Tagging of library documents, that are already in the stock of the library, with RFID tags, can be either outsourced to a vendor or done in house by the library staff. The decision has to be taken keeping into consideration the total collection, time factor and the cost factor.

All the selected libraries had arranged presentations from the vendors about the RFID technology. Before implementing RFID technology in their respective libraries 55.5% visited other libraries which had implemented this technology to see how the system was working. 77.8% libraries invited tenders for the supply, testing and installation of RFID technology. During discussion with the librarians, it was found that some of the eligibility criteria for participating in the tender document included company's presence in India for a certain number of years, 3-5 library installation sites, Original Equipment Manufacturer (OEM) of RFID hardware components or an authorized distributor of OEM of RFID hardware component or a system integrator having experience in RFID solutions, etc. 66.7% libraries mentioned that before going for full scale RFID implementation, they carried out a pilot project for about 1000-5000 books to know how the RFID system works in a library, different types of problems faced, create awareness amongst the library staff about the technology, etc. The main objective for running pilot project was to fix the problems encountered initially so that the project gets implemented within time and staff also gets some experience. All the selected institutions reported that the vendors had provided training for installation and use of RFID components. Retrospective tagging of library documents is a very tedious and time consuming process. Regarding the retrospective conversion of tagging of library documents, 55.5% libraries reported that both the RFID vendors and the library staff carried out this work whereas in some of the libraries it was done by the library staff.

4.5.4. Training/ support

During the implementation stage, it is vital to keep library staff up to date on what is going on. Vendors give onsite training on how to use different components of RFID, how to paste RFID tags on the books, how to do programming of RFID tags, how to take data form Library Management Software before doing inventory check etc. Once the system has been implemented, it is necessary to have the support service from the vendors for smooth functioning of RFID technology. Support service from the vendors at the right time and at the right place is a critical factor for the effectiveness and sustainability of RFID technology. Vendors generally provide support service 'on-site' as well 'on-call' and also provide continued R & D and software updates, live support service through Internet, etc. On the satisfaction level of librarians about the training and support provided by the RFID vendor most of them were moderately satisfied with the training and support provided by the vendors.

4.6. PRESENT STATUS OF RFID TECHNOLOGY

4.6.1. Networking system

Libraries use different kinds of network (i.e., LAN and Wi-Fi) for communication between RFID components and LMS. Local Area Network (LAN) is the most important set-up, which is used to provide a wider access to the library services at a very high speed. The analysis reveals that 66.7% libraries are using LAN for communication between RFID components and LMS, whereas 22.2% libraries have Wi-Fi network for communication between LMS and RFID hardware and software. Only one library (i.e., IIT, Roorkee) is using both types of networks (i.e., LAN as well as Wi-Fi) for communication. It is clear from the data above that LAN has been preferred by the libraries over Wi-Fi network because of its speed, security, reliability, range, etc. The only advantage of having Wi- Fi networking is that if one wants to move or change the position of the RFID components, there is no need for extra wires/ cables to connect it to the network.

4.6.2. Library Automation Software and RFID Protocol

It is a futile exercise to think about the RFID technology without the Library Management Software as it is the heart of an RFID application system. It is the communication gateway among the various components of the RFID system. It receives the information from one or more of the readers and exchanges information with the library database. RFID-LMS integration is essential for successful implementation of RFID. Most RFID systems used the SIP2 /NCIP protocol to communicate with the library management system. If LMS does not have these protocols, then either it needs to be modified to include the SIP2/NCIP protocol or the library has to switch over to other LMS which supports these protocols.

A large number of libraries (i.e., 77.8%) have adopted “Libsys” software which is developed by the LIBSYS Ltd,

Gurgoan. It was also observed during the visit to the libraries that most of the libraries which are using LibSys software in their respective libraries are using LSmart RFID solution (offered by the Libsys Corporation) for all the RFID operations comprising of tagging, circulation, self checkout and check-in, inventory control, etc. The libraries that have LMS software that did neither has SIP2 nor NCIP protocol required for communication with RFID components have either to shift to new software or use it with some customization as per the requirements of the library.

LMS-RFID Integration is a key to success for implementation of RFID in libraries and it require a communication protocol or standard to connect RFID components like Self-Check out/check-in, Book Drop, etc. and LMS systems. Presently, there are two main protocols (i.e., SIP2 and NCIP) which are available to facilitate communication between RFID and LMS. SIP was originally developed by 3M® to enable communication between their original Self-Service unit and LMS. Whereas SIP operates within a single library, NCIP offers the ability to extend circulation to library consortia and also support inter-library loan. It is clear from the above table that all the libraries i.e, 100% use SIP 2 protocol for communication between LMS and RFID components.

4.6.3. RFID Components

As explained in detail earlier in Chapter1 the basic components of an RFID system are:

- Tags
- Reader
- Antenna
- Host computer with appropriate application software

RFID tags are tiny microchips with memory and an antenna coil, thinner than paper and some only 0.3 mm across. There are two types of RFID tags—passive and active. The radio waves that are transmitted by an antenna interact with an integrated circuit embedded on an RFID tag that in turn sends back these waves to a reader. The reader then converts those waves into digital information that instantly identifies the item that responds. The RF energy from the reader antenna is received by the RFID tag antenna and is used to power up the microchip.

There are 4 major frequency ranges that RFID systems operate at.

- Low Frequency (LF) 125 to 148 KHz
- High Frequency (HF) 13.56 MHz
- Ultra High Frequency (UHF) 915 MHz
- Microwave 2.45 GHz

Low-frequency systems are generally distinguished by short reading ranges, slow read speeds, and lower cost. Higher-frequency RFID systems are used where longer read ranges and fast reading speeds are required, such as for vehicle tracking and automated toll collection. Microwave requires the use of active RFID tags.

44.44% of libraries under study had tagged more than 2.5 lakh volumes of their collection, 22.22% had tagged more than one lakh volumes and the rest 33.33% less than one lakh. 77.8% have both Self-check-out and Self-check-in/book drop system (which allow patrons to check out/check-in items without any assistance from the library staff) in their respective libraries. Only 22.22% libraries do not have Self-check-out/ check-in system in their respective libraries. In these institutions, circulation work is being performed by library staff with the use of RFID system only at the staff end. All the libraries have staff workstations. Conveyor and sorting systems, that can move library material and arrange them by category into separate bins or onto separate carts, are not being used by any of the libraries so far.

66.7% of the participating libraries have Digital Library Assistant/Shelf Management Reader that assist in shelf reading and inventory control without having to remove items from the shelves as is necessary when doing an inventory on bar coded items.

4.6.4. RFID Tags

All the surveyed libraries are using passive, High Frequency (HF) tags which operate at 13.56 MHz band. Longevity or life expectancy of RFID tag is another important concern while selecting the RFID tags because a book may be issued several times and may live on a shelf for several years. Hence, it needs to have a tag which is reliable over a much longer span. The chip in the RFID tag normally has a projected life expectancy usually measured in "cycles" which indicates how many read/ write operations can be expected to be completed successfully before its failure. About the life expectancy of the RFID tag being used by the libraries it is clear that 44.4% libraries have used RFID tags which have a life time guarantee, 33.3% have used those RFID tags which have a guarantee for 10 years, whereas 22.2% have used RFID tags which have a guarantee for 25 years.

4.6.5. RFID Standards

Understanding RFID standards helps one to determine the best solution to one's business needs and gives one insight into how the industry is regulated. This is as important as to know the different types of RFID systems. RFID standards are guidelines or specifications for product development and use as in the case of any other industry. There are standards that provide guidelines about how RFID systems work, how data is transferred, what frequencies they operate at and how communication works between the reader and the tag. To ensure that products are interoperable, regardless of the vendor or user, RFID standards help.

66.7% libraries under study are using RFID tags which are ISO 15693 standard compliant, whereas only

22.2% are using RFID tags which are both ISO 15693 and ISO 18000-3 compliant. Only one library is using RFID tags which are ISO 18000-3 compliant only.

During the interview with the librarians, they were asked about the reason for choosing a particular RFID standard. Some of them informed that the data standard which their RFID supplier has proposed was adopted by them. As all the libraries selected under study have implemented RFID technology before the publication of ISO 28560 (i.e., before April 2011), they are using a proprietary data model, i.e., their present system may not be interoperable with other RFID vendors. They also informed that some RFID suppliers are now claiming to be able to read any tag format which at first glance may seem like an excellent solution similar to barcode systems. At present, RFID system used in the participating libraries is propriety in nature and will work as long as the RFID supplier continues to support the data model; otherwise they will have to migrate to a new standard.

4.6.6. Information Stored on RFID tag

The tiny RFID tags can store detailed information about an item. Because most libraries have library management IT systems, the data for the tags can be generated from the library's database. The data can include a number of fields such as the book's unique identifier, loan record and bar code number, etc. All the selected libraries reported that they had entered accession number of books on RFID tags. 33.3% mentioned that they had entered the title of the book as well as the author's name on the RFID tags whereas 22.2% indicated that they had entered the library code on the RFID tags. It is thus clear that all the libraries do enter the accession number of books on RFID tags, whereas very few libraries have entered any other bibliographic information on RFID tags.

During the discussions with the librarians/library

professionals the libraries it was observed that the tags used by most of them are "powerless", have a very small read range, store a minimum amount of data and carry no patron data on the tags. Patron loan information is stored only in the Integrated Library Management System. However, in order to read the RFID tag, one needs to obtain the required RFID based reader and its position and also gain access to the ILS to determine the title or other information of the tagged item.

4.6.7. Library collection tagged other than books

In all the libraries mostly the collection tagged is that of books. Only 22.2% libraries had tagged the current periodicals, the same percentage of libraries i.e., 22.2% had tagged bound volumes of journals. 44.4% libraries had tagged theses and only one library had tagged manuscripts. No library has tagged CD/DVDs. It is clear that other than books, very few libraries have tagged theses and current periodicals. When the librarians were asked as to why they have not tagged periodicals, theses, manuscript and CDs, most of them informed that such documents are not issued out to the users. Hence, there is no need to tag such items.

4.6.8. Digital Library Assistant/Shelf Management Reader

The Digital Library Assistant (DLA) is a cordless, handheld device that instantly reads RFID Tags on library materials, turning shelf-reading, shelving, sorting, searching, weeding and exception-finding into routine tasks. Compact and easy to use, the Digital Library Assistant can hold information on more than one million items. Digital Library Assistant/Shelf Management Reader provides technological solution to identify lost and missing books, proper shelf-arrangement and for doing inventory control. 66.7% libraries have Digital Library Assistant/ Shelf Management Reader, out of which some libraries are not using the same. The frequency of use of the DLA is very less in most of the libraries. 80% libraries are using

DLA for determining correct order of the books on the shelves. Many libraries use it for searching individual book/s requested by the users. However, it was clear that none of the participating library is using the DLA for inventory control.

4.7. BENEFITS REALISED AFTER IMPLEMENTING RFID

4.7.1. Circulation

The circulation of materials is the primary area in libraries where RFID is used. Rather than the barcode systems commonly in use in libraries RFID has a number of advantages.

In case of Barcode the user has to align the barcode with the infrared beam for the reader to read it. The Barcode systems used vary in how precise this presentation must be, and therefore it takes time to align the item for reading. RFID does not require any alignment. Items can be placed in any position across the check out pad and thus issue is relatively quickly.

Many of the libraries in the study desired to circulate more books with less staff. Many libraries that had started using their new or renovated facility with RFID reported an increase in circulation of the library material. This was attributed generally to the appeal of the new technology. What appealed to the libraries most was RFID's possibilities for faster check out for circulating materials and easy to learn self check-out so that they could do more perhaps even with less staff.

77.8% libraries observed reduction in queue at circulation desk /counter, 66.7% informed that library is now providing extended hours of circulation without additional staff. 77.8% indicated that with the implementation of RFID system, library staff is now free to provide more users' centric services. Also 77.8% indicated that it saves time of the library staff and reported that number of staff required to manage circulation desk has reduced. 55.5% indicated that with the implementation of RFID, circulation of library documents has increased.

4.7.2. Collection development

Collection development is a vital process in creating and building a library qualitatively. Collection development involves the identification, selection, acquisition, and evaluation of library resources for a community of users. Collection development is at the heart of the mission of libraries. It is in being able to meet the needs of individuals with the "right stuff". The various RFID components such as, Self-checkout / Book drop / DLA etc. provide usage statistics/ transaction reports etc. that can be used as a tool for optimal and qualitative selection/acquisition of library materials, thus making RFID helpful in collection development in libraries. 88.9% libraries are aware about the fact that RFID components do provide usage statistics/ transaction reports about the daily issue return, the most issued books, books which are reserved by maximum students, etc. However, 33.3% responded that they were not using such reports generated by RFID components as a tool for selection/acquisition of library material.

4.7.3. Increased Security

The RFID technology has great security capabilities. The barcode system provides only circulation capabilities, but to create an effective security system along with it some other technology must be used. RFID is an improvement over the barcode systems because the RFID tag interacts with both the security technology and the circulation system. The RFID tag has a security chip that is activated when the item is checked out. The security gates installed read the tags as the user exits the library and alarm is raised if items pass through the security gates that have not been deactivated i.e. if the item has not been issued.

For the past decade or more the "tattle-tape" solution was dominant but was found to be unsatisfactory. The point of concern was in terms of patron service and staff time. The accuracy level of the security gates of previous system was poor, leading to many false alarms. The staff was required to ask users to empty backpacks or bags in search of the source of the alarm because the alarm system could not identify correctly the offending item. When the alarm turned out to be false it was an embarrassing situation for both the user and for the library staff. With the RFID system, most libraries reported greater satisfaction with the accuracy of the security system (fewer false alarms). However, all the libraries i.e. 100% reported that with the implementation of RFID technology, library collection has become more secure.

4.7.4. Inventories

RFID systems offer the ability to perform inventory checking function quickly using hand-held scanners. It allows the library staff to perform an inventory check without removing items from the shelves as is required when doing an inventory manually or on barcoded items. For the inventory capability interaction between the RFID system and the library's Integrated Library System (ILS) is required. In some cases libraries needed upgrades to their ILS that would permit the RFID system to interact with the library database. Some libraries had bought the inventory taking equipment but had not begun using it. Some libraries were primarily interested in using RFID to inventory particularly the most active areas of their collections whereas others intended to perform full inventories using RFID.

Closely linked with this inventory function is the potential use of portable RFID assistants to find requested items that might have been misplaced. This capability is seen as an increased service to users as well as making it easier for staff to find the requested items. This could also result in savings in terms of time and also because the libraries can fulfill requests from their own collection rather than purchase duplicate copies or making requests to other libraries for the mis-shelved items. It can lead to potentially reduce the amount of staff time spent searching for items that are listed as on the shelves but cannot immediately be located.

4.7.5. Cost Reduction

Most of the libraries anticipated reduction of costs for circulation staff. Check-in of items by staff as well as self check-in was expected to be faster, and some libraries reported that the check- in with RFID equipment was more accurate than it had been with the barcode system. Libraries that anticipated a reduction in staff numbers deployed at the circulation desk were looking forward to redeploying staff in other areas of the library and providing a variety of enhanced user services. The staff was expected to be relieved of repetitive motions that shall be achieved through reduction in the frequency of staff used in checking out materials as the users themselves will be doing most of the check out.

4.8. PROBLEMS IN RFID ADOPTION AND ITS IMPLEMENTATION

4.8.1. Circulation

It is important to know various problems faced by the librarians with the use of RFID components for circulation of library materials i.e., Self-Checkout/Check-in, Book Drop System, Security Gates, etc. 55.5% libraries informed that books returned through book drop get damaged more and the same percentage of librarians (i.e., 55.5%) felt that library staff has to perform the manual cross checking of books returned through book drop. 44.4% libraries faced problem of issuing multiple books at a time through self-check system. 33.3% libraries indicated that the users sometimes had complaints about the books or other documents which do not have the RFID tags, as in many libraries the complete collection has not been tagged yet. 33.3% libraries faced problems where bibliographic details of the books were not entered correctly in the RFID tag. No librarian has mentioned that he/she has ever faced problem of issuing or returning books in other than English language through RFID. 55.5% libraries did face problem of removal of RFID tags by the users whereas 44.4% also faced problem of false alarm near the security gate.

4.8.2. Digital Library Assistant

All the libraries are using Digital Library Assistant for various functions, such as to find missing books or for doing proper shelving of books. However, many reported that DLA does not read very thin books lying on the shelves. 40% informed that while using Digital Library Assistant one has to scan a shelf a number of times to get accuracy, but none of the librarians felt that DLA is complicated to use. However, during the interviews with the librarians/library staff, it was noted that most of them do not use the DLA because it is quite expensive, or was presently not working and the semi-professional and non professional staff does not want to use it because of the fear of damaging it.

4.8.3. Expensive solution

The barcode technology that has been fairly standard in libraries for nearly two decades is cheaper technology than RFID. RFID is an expensive solution as compared to the previous technology. Each library is unique in terms of their pre-RFID systems, in terms of the needs of the community that they serve and in terms of their goals for purchasing a new system. It is very difficult to generalize about costs and the benefits for each institution that result in cost savings. In thinking about whether to implement a new system such as RFID, libraries need to ask themselves what the costs and benefits will be compared to their present situation. Every institution has to make its own cost and benefit analysis before deciding to go in for the RFID technology.

4.8.4. Tagging/ Conversion

The time to tag the items in a library collection varied from library to library. Some libraries felt that it took a lot of time to get the item from the shelf to the tagging station, tag it and return it to the shelf. A number of libraries used the opportunity, to assess the item in hand for its condition and possible weeding, which led to lengthening the time spent on tagging per item. The jacketed books needed to have their jackets cut and then re-taped in order to allow the space to affix the tag in some libraries. Previously printing the barcode number and affixing the bar code on the item took very little time – approximately 5 seconds, whereas RFID tags have to be programmed and then fixed, and thus the time to tag one item with RFID tag varied from .33 minute to 2 minutes. The average time was just over 1 minute per item. The cost involved in terms of labor also varies greatly from library to library, depending upon how large the collection to be tagged was and also upon who did the tagging.

4.9. PROBLEMS FACED DURING RFID IMPLEMENTATION

There are many barriers to RFID adoption and its implementation in the libraries. Some of the barriers, as indicated in review of literature, include

- High cost of the technology
- Lack of senior management support
- Hesitance of staff towards implementation of new technology
- Lack of ICT expertise amongst library professionals
- Implementation challenges
- Compatibility with LMS
- Integration challenges

- Lack of proper RFID standards and protocols
- Lack of RFID vendors in India
- User privacy, etc.

88.9% libraries indicated "high cost" as the major barrier while implementing RFID technology. 55.5% highlighted "resistance from the staff" and "lack of RFID standards and protocols" as important problem in implementing RFID technology. 44.4% stated "lack of ICT expertise amongst library professionals" and "LMS- RFID Integration" as barriers in implementing RFID technology in libraries. 33.3% indicated "Lack of management support" and the same number of librarians felt "lack of RFID vendors in India" as a problem in RFID implementation. Only 22.2% mentioned that "user privacy" is a problem while implementing RFID technology in their respective libraries.

4.10. SATISFACTION LEVEL WITH THE RFID TECHNOLOGY

Majority of the librarians opined that implementation of RFID technology is very favorable in libraries. Implementing RFID technology requires great efforts, proper planning and huge funds. 44.4% are fully satisfied while the same percentage of librarians i.e., 44.4% is satisfied with this technology. However, only one of the librarians was very dissatisfied with the technology. When he was asked about the reasons of his dissatisfaction with RFID technology he stated that the decision of implementing RFID by his predecessor was wrong because of the huge amount involved in the purchase of RFID components, non use of the same due to scarcity of staff and monopoly of the vendor. However, overwhelming number of librarians selected for the present study were noted to be satisfied with the RFID technology and recommended the use of RFID technology to other libraries.

4.11. RFID IN LIBRARIES: USER PERSPECTIVE

As per the data collected from the four university libraries and two IITs libraries, there were around 56113 users enrolled during the period of study. The population of the study comprised faculty members, research scholars, post graduate and under graduate students of four universities and two IITs situated in Northern region of India. Simple random sampling technique was used. The total sample size was 1122 which is 2% of the total population of each institution covered in the study.

Libraries have a history of embracing new technologies to improve access to collections and services for customers. New technology always seems to be a hot topic in the library world. As library collections and the number of users grow, library staff often faces increasing demands and there is not enough time to have any kind of quality interaction with them. Technology is the key in approaching these ends, and enhancing the relationship of a library with its users and its staff. One of the main goals of adopting the RFID technology by libraries is user satisfaction and providing better services to them. In order to assess the required information about the awareness, use and perception about RFID technology from the users of the libraries selected under the study, the data was collected through questionnaire which was circulated amongst faculty members, research scholars, post-graduate and under-graduate students. The collected data was analyzed and interpreted institution wise and wherever necessary category wise keeping in view the objectives of the study. The data has been presented, compared and analyzed with the help of tables, figures and statistical measures.

The chapter deals with the analysis of the general information of the respondents like age, sex, gender, discipline, frequency and purpose of library visit; awareness of RFID components and user orientation programme; use of RFID components; problems faced;

users' perception and users' satisfaction by percentile method. Respondents from different categories and disciplines were selected to get a broader point of view i.e. faculty members (5.6%), research scholars (20.3%), post graduate students (42.4%) and undergraduate students (31.8%); from Basic Sciences (23.2%), Applied Sciences (28.9%), Social Sciences (32.5%) and Arts and Humanities (15.4%). 59.8% were male respondents and 40.2% were female respondents.

4.11.1. Frequency and purpose of Library Visit

The study shows that 92% visit their respective libraries regularly (daily, weekly, fortnightly, monthly and several times in a year) and only 8% visit the library occasionally. It shows a consistency in users' visit in all the libraries under study. Further analysis of data shows that the frequency of library visit is almost similar in individual academic library.

The main purpose of library visit as reported by the users in their respective libraries is for preparation of examinations, followed by for getting the library material issued/returned. To use digital library, to gain current awareness and to keep up-to-date and to use Wi-Fi facility has also been ranked high as the purpose of library visit. The users also visited to read newspapers and magazines, to consult periodicals and journals, to use theses and dissertations. It is clear that users mostly visit their respective libraries mainly for preparation of examination and for issue/return of the library material.

4.11.2. Awareness about the RFID Components and Facility

Library RFID system consist of various components, i.e., Self Check out (automated system for self issue of documents), Book Drop (automated system for self return of documents), Security gates and RFID tags. In order to know the awareness about these RFID components in the selected libraries under the study, respondents were asked to rate their level of awareness. Mostly the users became aware of RFID facility through librarian's guidance; however, some users became aware about RFID facility through their friends. Many users became aware of RFID facility when they went to the library to get the book issued/returned, very few came to know about this facility through library website and workshops/ seminars conducted by the libraries respectively. It is clear that majority of the users became aware of RFID through their friends/colleagues, while least number of users became aware of this facility through workshops / seminars conducted by their respective libraries. The study reveals that majority of the users are overall aware of Self-checkout system, Book drop system, Security gates either extremely, or moderately, or somewhat, or slightly.

4.11.3. Self - Checkout system

32.5% of users are extremely aware of Self-check out system, 26% of users are moderately aware, 16.4% are somewhat aware, 17.7% of users are slightly aware and only 7.3% of users are not at all aware of Self-check out system in their respective libraries.

50.5% users always or often use the Self check out system the rest used it only sometime or never. Further analysis of data shows that the overall frequency of use of Self check system is higher in the libraries where Self-checkout system is kept outside the circulation counter and the users are allowed to get the books issued at their end. It was observed that some libraries are using barcode enabled library card for the users as they felt that it is not secure to allow users to use the Self- checkout system unsupervised with such cards. To make Self-checkout system secure at the users end, library should plan to use RFID enabled library card or biometric system to make this facility functional at the users' end.

4.11.4. Book Drop system

94.9% of users are overall aware of Book drop system (either extremely, or moderately, or somewhat, or slightly), whereas only 5.1% users are not aware of it at all.

84% users use Book drop system always, often or sometimes. Further analysis of data shows that overall awareness about Book drop system is almost similar in individual libraries. Only 16% have either used it rarely or never in their respective libraries. Further analysis of data shows that the overall frequency of use of Book drop system is slightly higher in the libraries where the Book drop facility is operational 24/7 as compared to other participating libraries.

4.11.5. RFID Tags

Overall awareness of RFID tags is high, whereas only a small percentage of users are not aware of it at all. Further analysis of data shows that percentage of overall awareness about RFID tags is higher in IITs than in the university libraries. This may be due to the fact that students of IITs are technology savvy and they are familiar about this technology as they are the students of B.Tech, M.Tech, etc. Another reason may be that in IIT, the library staff has provided proper orientation about this technology to its users.

4.11.6. Security Gates

Most of the users were aware of the Security Gates available at the entrance of the library. Only 5.5% are not at all aware of Security gates in their respective libraries.

4.12. PROBLEMS FACED WHILE USING RFID COMPONENTS AND SOLUTIONS

The major problem faced by the users with the use of RFID technology was false alarm at the security gate and missing out a particular document while issuing multiple documents at a time. Another problem which was highlighted by the users while using RFID facility was that the issue/return slip printer not working or the tag was missing from documents/multimedia items. Slow speed of RFID system and wrong bibliographic details of the documents entered in RFID tag was also mentioned. Book returned but still showing in account was reported as the minor problem while using RFID facility by the users of all the libraries selected under the study.

4.12.1. Available solutions to the problems faced while using RFID components

Majority of the users go to the circulation desk for issue/return, while least number of users use online screen help when they face any problem while using Self-checkout /Book drop RFID system. Some users either ask the library staff or ask friends for assistance. Some also leave the documents when they face any problem while using RFID components rather than ask anyone.

4.12.2. User orientation programme

The libraries selected under study are regularly conducting the user education programmes to make their users familiar with RFID and its use in their respective libraries. The study reveals that in all the participating libraries, users are not much aware of the orientation programmes being conducted by their respective libraries about RFID and its use. However, the percentage of awareness of user orientation programme is slightly higher in IITs as compared to the university libraries.

4.12.3. Users' perception on implementation of RFID technology in libraries

In order to assess the usefulness of implementing the RFID technology in libraries the perception of the users as to the improvement in the services being provided by the libraries has to be taken into account.

4.12.4. Effective issue/return service

Majority of the users i.e. 76.1% agreed that with the implementation of RFID technology, issue/return service has became more effective

4.12.5. Simplification of issue/return service

Majority of the users (72.5%) agree with the opinion that with the implementation of RFID technology Issue/ return service has been simplified. However, very few users (6.9%) disagree with this opinion. It is clear from the study that there are minor variations amongst the opinion of the users (strongly agree and agree) regarding the statement that "with the implementation of RFID technology, issue/return service has been simplified" in all the libraries under study.

4.12.5. Improvement in Library image

It is clear from the study that majority of the users (72.5%) agree with the opinion that "with the implementation of RFID technology, library has improved its image among its users. However, very few users (10.1%) disagree with it. It is also clear that there are minor variations amongst the opinion of the users (strongly agree and agree) regarding "with the implementation of RFID technology, library has improved its image among its users" in the libraries under study.

4.12.6. Amount of time involved in issue/return

The opinion of users about the reduction in amount of time required to perform issue/return work with the implementation of RFID technology it is clear 64.5% agree with the opinion, however, 15.6% disagree with it. Data gathered also reveals that there are variations amongst the opinion of the users regarding amount of time required to perform issue/return work being reduced in the libraries after the implementation of RFID technology.

4.12.7. Extended circulation hours

The opinion of users about the benefit of extended circulation hours with the implementation of RFID technology was that 50% agree with the opinion that with the implementation of RFID technology, users can issue/return books beyond library circulation hours. However, 25.1% users disagree with it.

4.12.8. Issue/return of documents without taking assistance of library staff

It is clear from the study that 55.1% agree with the opinion that with the implementation of RFID technology, they can issue/return documents themselves without taking assistance of library staff. However, 20.9% disagree with it.

4.12.9. Improved shelf arrangement and Easy retrieval of documents

41.9% users agreed with the opinion that with the implementation of RFID technology, books on the shelves are now in proper order and allow easy retrieval of documents However, 26.8% disagree with it.

4.12.10. Overall ease of use and Satisfaction level with RFID system

The data analysis shows that 72.7% opined that RFID system is easy (very easy and easy) to use and a very few users i.e. 9.2% opined that it is difficult (very difficult, difficult) to use. Majority of users i.e. 67.3% are satisfied (fully satisfied, satisfied) with the RFID system, whereas very few i.e. 8.3% are dissatisfied (fully dissatisfied, dissatisfied) with the RFID system.

4.12.11. Satisfaction level with the RFID System

The data analysis shows that majority of users 67.3% are satisfied (fully satisfied, satisfied) with the RFID system, whereas a very few 8.3% are dissatisfied (fully dissatisfied, dissatisfied) with the RFID system.

4.13. CONCLUSION

The analysis of data shows that the top management support and perceived RFID benifits was the key factors for RFID adoption in all the selected libraries in Northern India. The study reveals that the most preferred purpose for implementing RFID technology in all the selected libraries was Self- issue/return and faster issue /return. The study shows that all the nine selected libraries in Northern India are in the initial stages of RFID implementation and they are realizing benefits; reduction in queue at circulation desk /counter, extended hours of circulation without additional staff, library staff is now free to provide more users' centric services, number of staff required to manage circulation desk has reduced, library collection has become more secure, etc. after implementing RFID technology. At the same time library staff is also facing some problems i.e., problem of removal of RFID tags by the users, manual cross checking of books, books returned through Book drop get damaged more, etc. with the use of RFID technology. It is found in the present study that majority of librarians indicated "high cost", resistance from the staff and "lack of proper RFID standards and protocols" as a major barrier in implementing RFID technology in libraries. The present study reveals that majority of librarians are satisfied with the implementation of RFID technology in their respective libraries and recommended RFID implementation in libraries. The study recommends that all the libraries under the study should use RFID technology as a tool for stock verification and a collection development.

The study reveals that users are almost aware of RFID components and using it almost regularly. It is found in the present study that users are facing some problems while using RFID technology in all the libraries selected under study. The major problem that they face are false alarm at the security gate as well as issuing multiple document at a time. Therefore, to overcome with these problem librarians should discuss security gate positioning and tag detection rates with the suppliers. The present study reveals that majority of the users are satisfied with the implementation of RFID technology in libraries. It is also found in the study that majority of the users are not much aware of the orientation programme being conducted by their respective libraries about RFID and its use. Therefore, it is strongly recommended that all the libraries need to organise such programmes more frequently to familiarise their users with RFID technology and its use.

5

Implementing RFID in Libraries: Practical Suggestions

Implementing RFID effectively in the libraries is a big challenge task for the librarians. Based on experience on the recent RFID implementations in libraries and information centers in Northern Indian Libraries, suggestions were provided to overcome the practical glitches faced by the libraries that have already implemented the technology. Successful implementation and smooth functioning of RFID in libraries involves the following recommendations:

- Although all the libraries organise user orientation programme, yet it is evident from the present study that majority of users are not much aware of the orientation programme being conducted by their respective libraries about RFID and its use. Therefore, it is strongly recommended that all the libraries need to organise such programmes more frequently to familiarise their users with RFID technology and its use. It is also suggested that all the libraries need to arrange lectures/ tutorials/ demonstrations /workshops/ seminars on RFID more frequently.

- Since it is been observed that use of Digital Library Assistant is very low in libraries, it is suggested that DLA must be used at least on daily/weekly basis in these libraries for determining correct order of the books on the shelves, finding reservations, missing books, stock verification, etc.
- Although majority of libraries do have a recurring budget provision for AMC of RFID hardware/ software and purchase of new RFID tags, yet the amount is quite low. Therefore, it is suggested that all the libraries should have a proper budgetary provision for AMC of RFID Hardware/Software and purchase of new RFID tags in their library budget with an increase of 5-10% annually.
- None of the libraries selected under the study have RFID conveyor and sorting system so far. Therefore, it is suggested that in future, libraries should purchase this system depending upon the budget, staff shortage, etc.
- All the libraries selected under the study have implemented RFID technology before the publication of ISO 28560 (i.e., before April 2011). They are using a proprietary data model, i.e., their present system may not be interoperable with other RFID vendors. Therefore, it is suggested that the libraries which are planning to implement RFID in their libraries must use RFID tags that are ISO 28560 complient in addition to ISO 15693, ISO 18000-3 and other global standards and protocols given by NISO.
- None of the libraries selected under study considered RFID technology as a tool for collection development in their respective libraries. Therefore, it is suggested that all the libraries should use RFID technology

for collection development as well.

- In the present study, users highlighted false alarm at the security gates as their main problem with RFID. This problem could be due to presence of metal gates, size of the antenna positioned at security gates, quality of tags and readers,presence of electronic device near security gates or when the users carry multiple books and passes through security gates. To overcome the problem of false alarm at the security gates, it is suggested that the librarians should discuss security gate positioning and tag detection rates with the suppliers. It is recommended that security gates should be placed at least 3-4 feet away from metal door frames and 8-10 feet away from computers. It is also recommended that gates should be covered with wooden frames to avoid metal interference.
- To overcome the problem of scanning very thin books through DLA, it is suggested that RFID tag should be pasted near the spine label and at different positions if inside the back cover. Libraries may use wooden shelves instead of metal shelves to avoid metal interference while scanning the books using DLA.
- To overcome the problem of power failure, it is suggested that all the libraries should have UPS connected to all the RFID components and ILS server. They may also have generator facility or any other backup system to run the RFID system smoothly in case of power failure.
- While doing retrospective tagging of library collection, it is suggested that library staff should use some method of marking the tagged collection so that these can be easily identified. It will save the time of the library staff to identify the untagged documents. Retrospective tagging of library collection can be

carried out on rent or lease programming stations from the vendors.

- It is also suggested that during the retrospective tagging of library collections, books returned through circulation counter without a tag must be tagged before being returned to the shelves.
- It is suggested that the libraries which are in the process of implementation of RFID should first tag those documents which are more in circulation.
- It is suggested that staff members should be deputed at or near the Self-check system/Book drop system to provide users assistance to the users.
- Regarding protection of user privacy, libraries should follow ALA guidelines and store no personal information on RFID tags. It is also suggested that libraries should only store accession number of the document on RFID tags as storing additional information of the documents (i.e., title, author, ISBN etc.) of the books will slow the programming operation and also has potential for compromising patron privacy.
- It is suggested that libraries should use the most secure connection for communications between LMS and RFID components to prevent unauthorized monitoring and access to personally identifiable information.
- It is also recommended that libraries should continue to use barcode along with RFID tags on the books as bar codes are required for inter-library loan and also for programming RFID tags, the scanning of bar code is the most accurate and fastest method as compared to manual entry of accession number on RFID tags.
- It is also suggested that libraries should provide SMS alert service to their users whenever they issue/return/reserve booksthrough RFID system.

- To overcome the major problem of removal of RFID tags by the users, it is suggested that RFID tags should be covered with book pocket or libraries should hide it by pasting a white paper on it.
- Although the user can get the documents check-in/out themselves, yet for paying the fine they have to come to the circulation section, it is suggested that librarians should discuss with their RFID supplier to either integrate self-pay fine system with self-check out system or have separate payment stations. This will allow users to pay their fine through credit cards\ cash without going to the circulation counter.
- It is suggested that libraries should ask RFID suppliers about the RFID tag life expectancy to ensure that RFID tags should have adequate re-write cycles and durability.
- It is recommended that libraries should discuss with book vendors/distributors to supply new books already tagged at no extra cost. This will save recurring expenses of purchasing new tags.
- It is recommended that smaller and new libraries should adopt RFID at an early stage since initial costs and resources involved in adoption and implementation of this technology is lower as compared to significant benefits it provides.

6

NFC: An Alternative to RFID in Libraries

Similar to other identification technologies such as RFID, barcodes and QR codes, the Near Field Communication (NFC) is a wireless communication technology that uses invisible radio waves to identify an object from a short distance i.e. up to 20 cm using 13.56 MHZ frequency. NFC is a short-range wireless technology having only a few centimetres of communication distance. It is based on the existing 13.56 MHZ RFID contactless card standards which have been established for several years and are used for payment, ticketing, electronic passport and access control among many other applications. Data rates start at 106 kilobits per second and go up to 424 kilobits per second. A few NFC devices are already capable of supporting up to 848 kilobits per second which is now being considered for inclusion in the NFC Forum specifications. [130] Compared to other wireless communication technologies NFC is designed for proximity or short-range communication which provides a dedicated read zone and some inherent security.Its frequency band is 13.56 MHZ therefore it falls into the ISM band which is available worldwide. It is a bi-directional communication meaning that you can exchange data in both directions with a typical range of 4-10 cm depending on the antenna geometry and the output power. With the smart phone normally used, one will get less range than with a dedicated reader device due to a lower output power.[131 132]

6.1. DIFFERENCE BETWEEN RFID AND NFC TECHNOLOGY

Both RFID and NFC technologies are similar in that both use Radio waves. However, NFC can be said to have evolved from the Radio-Frequency Identification (RFID) standards and can actually be taken as an extended form or a subcategory of RFID. Both RFID and NFC technologies communicate to exchange data within electronic devices in active mode, as well as, in passive mode. In the active mode outgoing signals are basically those that actually come from the power source, whereas in case of passive mode the signals use the reflected energy they have received from the active signal. In RFID technology the radio waves can send information to receivers up to a fairly large distance. If provided with high amount of power, these signals can also be sent to extreme distances e.g. in the case of airport radar. RFID is also used very often in tracking animals and vehicles.

If we look at the other side of the spectrum, items like passports and payment cards if they have long distance transmissions they could be misused. It would be a bad idea as it involves the risk of someone stealing your personal information or funds.[133] NFC tags are very small in size so as to fit on the inner side of devices and products such as inside luggage, purses and packs as well as from inside wallets and clothing and can be tracked. NFC technology has added security features that make it much more secure than the previously popular RFID equivalent and it is difficult to steal information stored in it. NFC has short range of work area compared to other wireless technologies, so it can be widely used for payments, ticketing and service admittance and thus has proved to be a safer technology. It is because of this security feature that this technology is used the cellular phones to turn them into a wallet.[134]

Both the wireless technologies of RFID and NFC can operate in both modes i.e. active and passive communication modes, to exchange data within electronic devices. The main differences between NFC and RFID [135] are:

- Although both RFID and NFC use radio frequencies for communication, NFC can said to be an extension of the RFID technology. The RFID technology has been in use for more than a decade, but NFC has emerged on the scene recently.
- RFID has a wider range whereas NFC has limited communication and operates only at close proximity. NFC typically has a range of a few cms.
- RFID can function in many frequencies and many standards are being used, but NFC requires only a fixed frequency of 13.56 MHz, and some other fixed specifications to function properly.
- RFID technology can be used for such applications as item tracking, toll plaza, vehicle movement etc. that require wide area signals. Whereas NFC is appropriate for the applications that carry data that needs to be kept secure like mobile payments, access control etc. that carry creditable information.
- RFID operates in a long distance range while exchanging data wirelessly so it is not secure for the applications that store personalised data. RFID using items susceptible to various fraud attacks such as data corruption. With NFC a solution for this problem has been found. NFC has a short working range that reduces this risk of data theft, eavesdropping and the middle man attacks up to a considerable level.

- NFC has the capability to communicate both ways and thus is suitable to be used for advanced interactions such as card emulation and peer-to-peer sharing
- A number of RFID tags can be scanned simultaneously. Whereas only a single NFC tag can be scanned at a time.

6.2. HOW NFC WORKS

The extended functionality of a traditional RFID system has led to the NFC Forum. It has defined three operating modes for NFC devices Tag reader/writer mode; peer-to-peer mode and card emulation mode. The NFC Forum technical specifications for the different operating modes are based on the ISO/IEC 18092 NFC IP-1, JIS X 6319-4 and ISO/IEC 14443. These specifications must be used to derive the full benefit from the capabilities of NFC technology. Contactless smart card standards are referred to as NFC-A, NFC-B and NFC-F in NFC Forum specifications.[136]

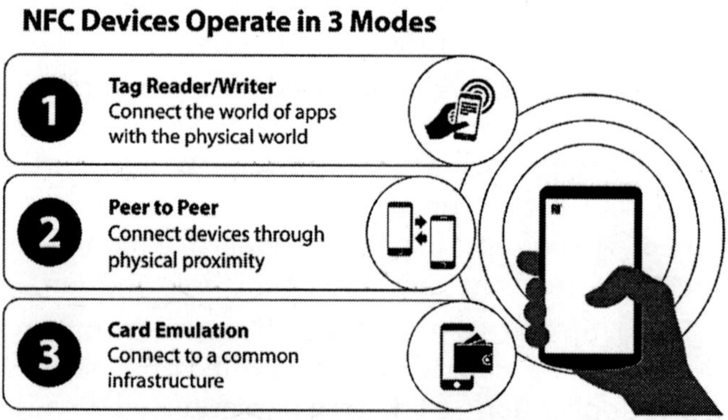

Fig. 6.1. How NFC works[136]

6.2.1. READER/WRITER MODE

In the reader/writer mode, the NFC-enabled device is capable of reading NFC Forum-mandated tag types, such as a tag embedded in an NFC smart poster. This mode enables NFC-enabled devices to read the information that is stored on NFC tags embedded in smart posters and displays. Since these tags are relatively inexpensive they provide a great marketing tool for companies.

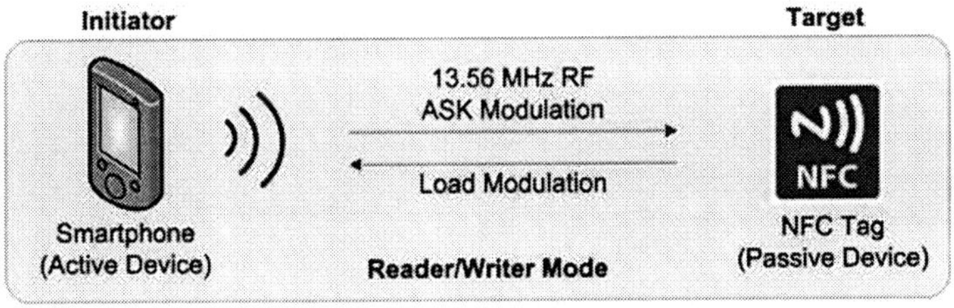

Fig. 6.2. Reader Mode[136]

The reader/writer mode on the Radio Frequency interface is compliant with the NFC-A, NFC-B and NFC-F schemes. Examples of its use are: in reading timetables, tapping for special offers, and updating frequent flyer points, etc.[136]

6.2.2. Peer-to-Peer mode

In Peer-to-peer mode both the devices must be NFC-enabled and then it allows them to communicate with each other to exchange information and to share files. The users of NFC-enabled devices can thus quickly share information and other files with a touch. As an example, users can set-up parameters, share Bluetooth or Wi Fi link or exchange such data such as digital photos or virtual business cards.

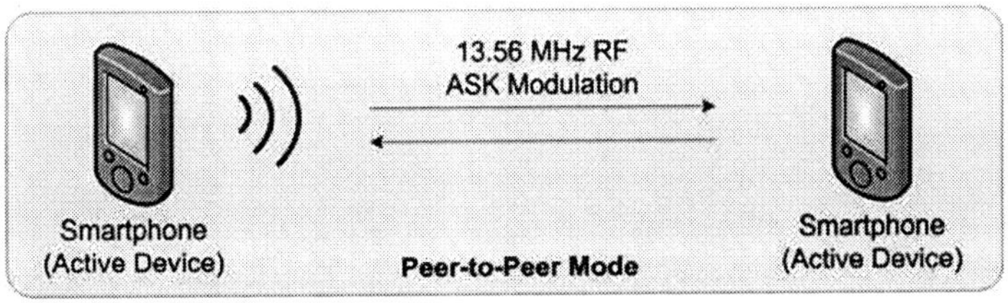

Fig. 6.3. Peer-to-Peer Mode[136]

Peer-to-peer mode is based on NFC Forum's Logical Link Control Protocol Specification and is standardized on the ISO/IEC 18092 standard.[136]

6.2.3. Card Emulation Mode

In card emulation mode an NFC device behaves like a contactless smart card. These devices act like smart cards, so that users can perform transactions with just a touch such as purchases, ticketing, and transit access control. An NFC device may have the ability to emulate more than one card. In Card Emulation Mode, the NFC-enabled device communicates with an external reader much like a traditional contactless smart card. This allows payments and ticketing contactlessly by NFC-enabled devices without changing the existing infrastructure.

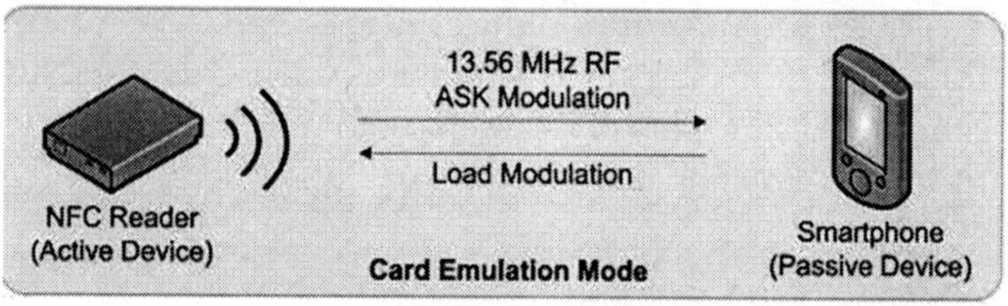

Fig. 6.4. Card Emulation Mode[136]

By adding NFC to a contactless infrastructure one can enable two-way communications. In the air transport sector, this could simplify many operations such as updating seat information while boarding, or adding frequent flyer points while making a payment.[137]

6.3. NFC STANDARDS AND SPECIFICATIONS

The NFC specifications are defined by an industry organization called the NFC Forum which has nearly 200 member companies. This Forum was formed in the year 2004 with the objective to advance the use of Near Field Communication Technology. This purpose was achieved by the Forum by educating the market about NFC technology and by developing specifications, ensuring interoperability among devices and services. The NFC Forum members are working together in task forces and working groups. As said earlier the NFC technology is based on existing 13.56 MHZ, RFID standards and includes several protocols such as ISO 14443 type A and type B, JIS X 6319-4 which is also a Japanese Industrial standard known as (Sony FeliCa). The ISO 15693 standard which is an additional 13.56 MHZ protocol established in the market for which the NFC Forum has a task force to integrate it into the NFC specifications. Smart phones in the market are already supporting the ISO 15693 protocol. These NFC specifications and especially the specifications for the extended NFC functionalities are again standardized by the international standard organizations like ISO/IEC ECMA and ETSI.[138 139]

Different companies working in the field i.e. NXP, Infineon and Sony pronounced standards ISO/IEC 14443 A, ISO/IEC 14443 B and JIS X6319-4 that are known as the RFID standards. The first ever NFC standard was ECMA 340, that was based on the Air Interface of ISO/IEC 14443A and JIS X6319-4. ECMA 340 adapted the ISO/IEC standard 18092. Simultaneously the major credit card companies like Europay, Mastercard, and Visa have introduced the payment standard EMVCo that are based on ISO/IEC 14443 A and ISO/IEC 14443 B. Both groups harmonised the air interfaces within the NFC Forum. They are named NFC-A (ISO/IEC 14443 A based), NFC-B (ISO/IEC 14443 B based) and NFC-F (FeliCa based).[140]

6.4. NFC TAGS

A Near Field Communication tag (NFC tag) is a small microchip embedded in a sticker or wristband that can be read by the mobile devices that are within range. Information regarding the item is stored in these microchips. This NFC tag has the capability to send the information stored on it to NFC enabled mobile phones. NFC tags can also perform various actions, such as changing the settings of handsets or even launch a website.

Mostly smart phones available in the market today have inbuilt NFC capabilities. The smart phone users can purchase NFC tags online. The tag memory capacity varies by the type of tag and thus the amount of information that can be stored on it various. For example, a tag may store a phone number or an URL. The most modern example of a common use of NFC tag function is the mobile wallet payment processing, where the user swipes or flicks a mobile phone on a NFC reader to make payment. Google's version of this system is Google Wallet.141

	NFC Forum Platform				
	Type 1 Tag NFC-A compliant	Type 2 Tag NFC-A compliant	Type 3 Tag NFC-F compliant	Type 4 Tag NFC-A, NFC-B compliant	Type 5 Tag NFC-V compliant
Compatible Products	Broadcom Topaz	NXP MIFARE Ultralight/ NXP MIFARE Ultralight C NXP NTAG 21x (F) NXP NTAG I2C	Sony FeliCa	NXP DESFire / NXP SmartMX-JCOP (MIFARE DESFire implementation) / ST Microelectronics	NXP ICODE SLI (x) / Texas Instruments Tag-it HF-I / EM423x / ST Microelectronics
Memory Size	454 Bytes	48 / 128 / 144 / 504 / 888 / 1904 Bytes	1, 4, 9 KBytes	2 / 4 / 8 KBytes / up to 144 Kbytes / 106 Kbytes	32 / 112 / 128 / 160 / 256 Bytes
Unit Price	Low	Low	High	Medium / High	Low / Medium
Data Access	Read/Write	Read/Write or Read-only	Read/Write or Read-only	Read/Write or Read-only	Read/Write
Active Content*	-	-	-	x / 0	-
Operation Specification	ISO/IEC 14443-3 A	ISO/IEC 14443-3 A	JIS 6319-4	ISO/IEC 14443-4 A/B	ISO/IEC 15693

*Active Content refers to the ability for a developer to store and run small applications (called 'cardlets') on the tag. Only the Type 4, non-DESFire tags have this ability, all other tags are treated as static storage device.
MIFARE Ultralight, NXP MIFARE Ultralight C, MIFARE DESFire, SmartMX, NXP ICODE SLI(x) are registered trademarks of NXP B.V.
Tag-it HF-I is a registered trademark of Texas Instruments
EM423(x) is a registered trademark of EM Microelectronic.

Fig. 6.5. A quick overview of the tag types[142]

6.5. APPLICATIONS OF NFC

Since it emerged as a standard technology in 2003, NFC technology has been implemented across multiple platforms in various ways. The primary driving force behind NFC is its application in the commercial sector in which the implementation of the technology focuses on such areas as sales and marketing. There are also emerging many new and interesting applications in various other fields of education and health care etc. All of these may impact libraries, librarians, and library users, either by prompting adaptations to existing collections and services or inspiring innovation in our profession.

- Mobile payment
- Access and authentication
- Transportation and ticketing

- Mobile marketing
- Healthcare
- Social media
- Gaming
- Inventory tracking, smart packaging, and shelf labels

6.5.1. Mobile Payment

The future of electronic payments will rely mostly on NFC technology. Near Field Communication is changing the way customers are making payments by turning smart phones into mobile wallets. Customers with NFC-enabled smart phones can link with their bank accounts and are able to pay by simply tapping phones to an NFC-enabled point-of-sale. This makes for a faster more secure transaction, customers get a receipt instantly on their phone creating an overall better shopping experience. With over 550 million NFC enabled smart phones expected to be in the market in 2015 and companies such as Google PayPal and now Apple, all having mobile wallet applications, this will lead to repeat sales. The need to accept NFC payments is greater than ever and businesses unable to accept NFC payments will lose business to those that do it.[143 144]

NFC is the new standard for smart phones for establishing radio communication. Once you have set up your critical details on your phone you can simply swipe your phone over the credit card reader and your payment will be processed instantly. For better security you can set up a password for all transactions or for transactions that exceed a certain preset value, for example if you set your limit to dollar 50, for any transaction above dollar 50 you'll instantly be asked to enter your password. Similarly if you lose your phone you can remotely wipe all the data in the phone which is a feature that comes in every Android phone. The biggest advantage is that you don't have to separately carry credit cards. You can use your cell phone which is always with you everywhere. Many new Nokia phones also have NFC feature including the Nokia C7. Besides payment, NFC can also be used for pairing with accessories and other devices. To start NFC payment system in the shops retailers must replace their existing credit card readers with credit card readers that have NFC chip built-in them, only then the smart phones shall be able to communicate with the payment system.[145]

6.5.2. Access and Authentication

A very familiar application of Near Field Communications today is "Keyless Access". NFC technology is a popular choice due to its features such as its convenience and ease of implementation. The auto detect feature of NFC and RFID tags can be used for access to restricted areas. For easier access to cars, other vehicles and doors the access keys, identification badges etc. can be replaced with NFC enabled device. One can imagine other potential uses of NFC in the future with the devices in the home being controlled by it. In the future when a person carrying a NFC-enabled phone passes a sensor in the driveway or at the gate, the house would unlock and the heating and lights would be on automatically. At present these functions are being performed via Wi-Fi, but using NFC they will be more secure and require much less power.[146]

6.5.3. Transportation and Ticketing

Hong Kong has the first-ever octopus mobile payment service which is enabled by the pilot launch of the octopus mobile. Simple three-two-one- you take a smart phone and insert a sim in the smart phone and you've got an octopus card. It's as simple as that and this is going to be very important for consumers, as we all know people want to get things done fast, so they are constantly looking for services which are convenient, effective and secure so as to protect the customers' money. This is the first mobile payment service enabled by Miss

WH Katie's Octopus mobile sim which in effect integrates the octopus functions that the consumers are used to with NFC i.e. Near Field Communications which is becoming standard on most of the smart phones being sold today. The concept is to integrate the octopus function into an NFC mobile phone that means now one doesn't need to carry two things when one goes out. One only needs to carry an NFC mobile phone that functions both as a mobile as well as the auto path payment and thus adds value function. This is a significant step because now the industry has been talking about the NFC function and people always ask what can be done with the NFC feature and how it will help. Understandably this is going to be widely adopted NFC function. The auto based payment function in the NFC means that on a day to day basis when one needs to do transportation retail payment one can use NFC mobile phone.

Transport area has been a great market for contactless service as it needs speed because pushing a lot of people through to get on a train or a bus or a plane speed is required and this is where NFC comes in. It's very convenient as the market for transport is huge and there's an existing base that has been built using contactless technology. Looking at the airline industry one can have tickets stored on one's phone, redeeming it to get on board, also at the same time updating one's loyalty points or using phone to access the lounge, paying for purchases at the airport all with a single device and with a single touch.

6.5.4. Mobile marketing

In the commercial sector, the focus of NFC implementation has been naturally on the NFC-based marketing and advertising. The use of NFC is quiet similar to QR codes in the simplest form of marketing. In order physically display the digital information contained on the NFC tags they can be embedded into the indoor and outdoor signage. On tapping their smart phone on an NFC-enabled smart poster, the customer can read a consumer review, visit a Web site, or even view a movie trailer. The QR codes perform only restricted functions, however, NFC tags can provide much more complex interactions than this simple action. NFC-enabled mobile marketing can be interactive and much more personalized and customized as with NFC a bidirectional exchange is possible, i.e. a mobile device may not only receive information from the tag but also interact with it. As an example, a user can tap an NFC-enabled smart poster to purchase ticket to an event or movie, save a coupon for future use to their device, or even get directions to an event or store location. Thus, NFC creates new possibilities for businesses to promote their products and events and interact with potential customers and provide them better service.

6.5.5. Healthcare

When most of us visit a hospital for the first time we feel like foreigners in a new country where we have been thrust and have no guidebook to navigate around. We are not familiar with the terminology that the hospital uses and thus find ourselves dependent on strangers for our basic needs. NFC can be used for storing and taking doctor appointments. Doctor or any medical practitioner can take photos with their mobile phones of a health problem such as in cases of skin diseases and upload it to automatically create user profile of patients. The NFC tags can be used to store details of our caregiver, next medical appointment or next visit due or to request an appointment or to download patient records and also to share individual requirements of the patient by swiping an NFC mobile phone over NFC tags installed in the patient home. These services could be availed by simply putting the mobile near the NFC tags. NFC hospital information system helps the staff to quickly access all the necessary patient records.

NFC speeds up processes inside hospitals by a pre check of records before they require treatment or to know if prescription of medicines is right for the patient. NFC can be used for tracking when the doctor visited a patient so as to prevent human errors such as someone forgetting to mark in the log that the patient was visited and prevents the doctors or attendants from giving medication to patients who have already received it but the information may not have been logged in the patient record.

Chemists and pharmacists can also quickly check and supply the required medicines. In order to further diminish the risk of side effects due to the patient being allergic to certain medicines or to identify when any doubt arises, a quick check of the patientrecords can be done before giving the required treatment or prescribing medicines to the patients. This will ensure that the recommendations made and treatment given is just right for the patient in question. NFC medical card and bracelet tag can store relevant up-to-date patient information like his health history, allergies, infectious diseases etc. Other information of the patient such as insurance, current medications, procedures etc can also be stored. The tag displays a patient's photo, full name, date of birth or any other critical medicals conditions or any medical symbols, etc. Any additional caution needed when treating a patient or prescriptions can be stored on it and then can be used as your scripture, just present the card while check-in and your medical history is already known to your doctor.

6.5.6. Social media

Social Media has revolutionized the world! As also, has the Near Field Communication (NFC) technology. Connecting consumers of say a restaurant, bar, or retail establishments with various social media platforms is one of the possible uses for NFC. The social media platforms like Facebook and Twitter can be used to help the organizations to increase the number of people that visit or join the establishment every day. Let's assume one is the owner of a restaurant so that when people "check-in" to the restaurant these people act as an endorsement and this helps to advertise the restaurant. This helps to attract those friends of these people who are nearby to visit or might persuade them to visit on a future occasion.[146] With the increased usage of social media the most effective way to advertise one's business is to use the NFC technology. With the NFC technology, one will not have to convince a customer to scan a QR code, he can get a pop up notification on his phone that will allow him to use the option of "check-in" or not, simply by placing his phone on the table. This makes it extremely easy for the cutomer as it requires almost no effort and thus the number of "check-ins", or "shares", will most likey increase in a dramatic fashion and is all free advertising for the business. And the increased foot fall from this high value but low cost advertising will make using NFC worth it.

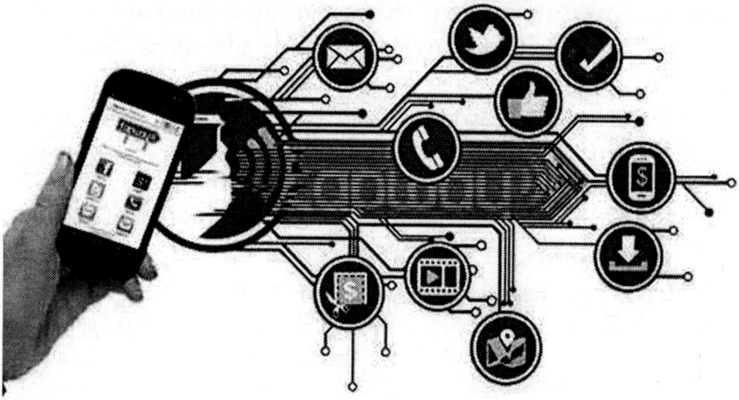

Fig. 6.6. NFC and Social Media[147]

6.5.7. Gaming

If you want to equip game elements such as figures and cards with additional digital features, or if you want to connect computer game features to real-world objects, then NFC technology is the bridge between physical and digital games. From soft toys with 'chips in their ears', to intelligent, high-tech playing cards, to secure gaming tokens – let your imagination run free. NFC enables one to use a favourite toy figure as an integral part of a video or mobile game experience by fusing video and mobile games with the physical world. NFC-enabled physical toys and collectables can act as active elements in console and mobile gaming, in an effortless and exciting way and extend authentic brand loop for licensed gaming merchandise. Players can tap each other's phones together and earn extra points or receive access to a new level, or get clues, by using NFC application.[148]

6.5.8. Inventory tracking, smart packaging, and shelf labels

Some implementations of smart packaging allow consumer access to inventory and tracking information that previously would only have been available to a manufacturer or product supplier. RFID technology has long been used in the commercial sector for inventory control and supply chain management. Smart packaging, of course, has uses beyond inventory control, and NFC-tagged objects could provide a wide variety of information in different use environments.

A variation on the idea of smart packaging is electronic shelf labeling, in which store shelves or displays rather than individual products bear NFC- enabled tags that customers may tap for additional information, such as up-to-date pricing. NFC-enabled smart phones can be used to tap the tags to access book reviews and information about the book's author and recommend the book to other readers. Users could check a book out or add it to a wish list to check out at a later date. Indeed, with NFC, library records and metadata could theoretically be stored on and retrieved from library physical holdings themselves, allowing a patron tap a book or resource borrowed from the library to recall its title, author, and due date.

A sector close to librarians' hearts is publishing and several publishers have started testing smart packaging for books, using embedded NFC tags to share additional content with readers such as book reviews, reading lists etc. With digital extras the concept of smart packaging has significant implications for libraries as a new opportunity to connect physical collections i.e. from books to digital media. One can envision in the future that a user when taps an NFC-enabled library book he shall get access to relevant digital information such as bibliographic information in a variety of citation formats, editorial reviews, the author's biography, a projected rating for the book based and links to similar other information.

6.6. APPLICATIONS OF NFC IN LIBRARIES

6.6.1. Borrowing and returning the books

Library is considered as heart of any institution and it is a place where the users can read, access and issue/ return the library collections. Due to the low cost of the barcode technology, most of the libraries around the world are using it for circulation management. However, the main constraints related to barcode technology are: it always requires a line-of-sight, does not provide security of library collection, does not offer any benefit for collection management and is becoming very difficult for the libraries to satisfy the increasing demands of the users. Thus comes up the need to implement new technology to improve the library circulation management, inventory and security of library collections. Librarians are always known as early adopters of technology and they have started using RFID to provide circulation services in a more effective and efficient manner, for security of library collections and to satisfy the increasing demands of the users.

Now libraries are using NFC technology as an alternative to RFID. Yusof, et al proposed a newly developed application called the "S-Library" that has adopted the Near Field Communication (NFC) technology.

S-Library stands for "Smart Library" in which library users can perform many library transactions just by using their mobile smart phones with integrated NFC technology. The users of S-Library are required to download and easily install an app in their compatible mobile phone. This app provides the user relevant and easy to use library functionality such as searching, borrowing, returning and viewing their transaction records. In this S-Library model the app is integrated with the Library Management Software. The S-library app needs to be installed on the mobile device, and the mobile device requires an Internet connection that will connect it to the LMS.

The S-Library provides five major functionalities to the user i.e. scan, search, borrow, return and transaction history. In the Scanning function users can access the information of a bookby simply touching their mobile phone to the NFC tag on the book. As soon as the phone will touch the book information regarding its title, author, contents, synopsis, etc., will automatically bc displayed on the screen of the mobile device. The users are allowed to perform the searching function to look for a book by entering keywords such as book title, author name, year etc. Through the borrowing function the app allows the users to borrow a book of his interest. The user just needs to touch his mobile phone to the NFC tagged book to borrow it. The transaction is automatically stored to the LMS database. Similar to the borrowing process is the returning process. The user is required to select the return function on the menu and touch the mobile device to the book, and the returning transaction will be automatically performed and stored in the LMS database. The user can check the due date for the current transaction as well as his transaction history. The function of transaction history allows the user to view the list of books that have been borrowed by him/her from time to time and their status.[149]

Data transmission for NFC technology is very high it can be up to 848 kb/s. Taking advantage of this high data rate, the response time for S-Library is also very fast. This is a huge improvement on RFID technology, where the data transmission rate is 484 kb/s, and especially on the barcode technology. In barcode technology the data transmission rate is variable and inconsistent as it depends wholly on the quality of the barcodes and poor quality of individual barcodes is a serious issue. The second key advantage of S-Library is that it has the set-up time of less than 0.1 min. The set-up time for RFID is also less than 0.1 min. but for the barcode equivalent it is more than 0.1 min. This proves that the NFC technology is a definite improvement over the traditional approaches. The third advantage of NFC is its usability in comparison to the other two technologies. The usability is human centric in NFC technology as it is intuitive and fast. In RFID and barcode technology usability is item centric.

All the shortcomings of RFID and barcode technology have been overcome by the S-Library. In the barcode technology, dependence was on quality of barcodes, printing clarity, print contrast ratio and also the there was the issue of low security level. RFID technology had the many drawbacks such as lack of common RFID standards, security vulnerability, reader and tag collision. NFC is based on the touch-based paradigm and is thus has presented a viable alternative tool for library users to overcome these weaknesses of the older technology.

Thus Yosof et.al[149] found that the advantages of S-Library are many. It resulted in some undisputed advantages as in faster book borrowing; saved time of the user as well as the library staff; the connection can be initialised in less than a second; no configuration required connecting to a mobile phone; higher user friendly ratings and high security are. However, there are some limitations of S-Library also. Firstly compatibility is an issue, because S-Library presently supports the android platform only. Secondly as this application can only support a range between 1-10 cm. distance coverage is an issue. Thirdly this application works only with android mobile phones that have integrated NFC technology in them. Finally, there is a small probability of the risk of the app crashing in future due to malicious software that could attack this application.

6.6.2. Mobile payment

Eventually the NFC technology can be used for performing several library functions such as making payments, paying library fines, purchasing tickets to library events, or donating to library fundraisers. Users may also be able to use their digital wallet to pay for photocopying, printing, scanning, etc. Keeping the requirements of the NFC technology in the future libraries have to enquire about the possibility of adding NFC payment capabilities into the existing hardware and also while purchasing new machines.

Already, Bibliotheca's Smartserv 1000 Self-serve kiosk, introduced in September 2013, includes NFC as a payment option. In the future other library automation companies for NFC integration would also be worth monitoring.[150]

6.6.3. Library Access and Authentication

These types of implementations suggest that NFC technology may play an important role in the next generation of identity management systems. Of particular interest in this context are several applications of NFC in two-factor authentication, which generally combine a physical, NFC-enabled component as well as a password or other digital credential. For example, an authentication system could require the user to type in a fixed password in addition to tapping an NFC-enabled phone, identity card, or ring. IBM has demonstrated a two-factor authentication method for mobile payment in which a user first types in a password and then taps an NFC- enabled credit card, issued by their bank, to their NFC- enabled smartphone.

Libraries could investigate similar access and authentication applications for NFC, both for internal use (staff badges and keys) as well as for public services. Particularly if NFC mobile payment finally gains consumer attraction, library patrons may begin to expect that they can use their NFC-enabled mobile devices to replace not just their credit cards but also their library cards. Already, D-Tech's RFID AIR Self Check unit allows library patrons to log into their user accounts by tapping their NFC-enabled phone to the kiosk. The patron then uses the kiosk's RFID reader to check out their library materials and receives a receipt via email or SMS. Beyond its application in circulation, NFC authentication can be applied to streamline access to other services and resources of the library. The users could be allowed to simply tap their NFC-enabled phone or contactless library card to log on to library computers, printers, and other hardware.[151] They could be used to make reservation of library spaces, classrooms, auditoriums or community halls, digital media labs, meeting rooms etc. Library users may use NFC authentication to be able to access digital library resources, such as databases, e journals, e books collections, and other digital collections. NFC might allow libraries of all kinds to provide more convenient access and authentication options to users, though privacy and security considerations would certainly need to be addressed. NFC access and authentication will certainly have an impact on academic libraries. At universities where NFC access systems are deployed, student identification cards can be replaced with NFC-enabled mobile phones for after-hours services such as library building entry, Wi-Fi access, and printing, copying, and scanning services. The inconvenience of multiple logins can be eliminated. However, the libraries will have to take the responsibility of protecting student information and library resources with added security.

6.6.4. Promotions of Library services

Librarians can borrow ideas from commercial implementations of NFC-based marketing to enhance promotions for library resources, services, and events. As a first step, NFC tags can complement several promotional uses of QR codes that have already been piloted or implemented in libraries. For promotional use, libraries can easily embed NFC tags in their new book displays that can be linked to the bestseller list or current acquisitions lists in the library catalog or digital collections. Similarly, if the reference book collection is tagged with NFC tags it could be linked to the relevant digital collections of databases or e books. NFC tags can be placed on library building doors or on library promotional material by which information such as library hours, opening days, schedule of events, membership rules or floor plans for the building could be shared. As an example, at the Renison University College Library, visitors can tap an NFC-enabled "library smartcard" to retrieve a digital brochure of library services in a variety of formats, including PDF, EPUB, and MP3.

To promote outreach programs and events instead of merely sharing links the libraries can take advantage of NFC's interactive capabilities. As an example, libraries could use NFC tags on their event posters so that the users that can scan them and register for an event, save the event to their personal calendar, join the Friends of the Library program, or even download a library app. To send a text message to a librarian the users can tap the smart poster promoting a virtual reference service. NFC-enabled promotional materials can engage users with library content even when they are outside of the library building itself. A brilliantly creative example that used NFC-enabled outdoor smart posters throughout the city to promote an exhibit of the 1893 World's Fair was that of

The Field Museum in Chicago. The posters of the event depicted a personage from 1893 from the back that invited the viewer to "See What They Saw." Users could tap their NFC-enabled mobile device to the smart poster (or read a QR code) to download an app from the Field Museum that included 360° images of the fair as well as videos highlighting items in the exhibition.[152]

6.6.5. For Inventory Control

The smart packaging use case brings forward a very important question for libraries that use RFID for inventory control. First, can existing RFID tags and infrastructure be leveraged to provide additional services to patrons with NFC-enabled mobile devices? The concept is not new; Walsh (2011)[153] envisioned using library RFID tags to store book recommendations or other digital information, which users could then access with a conveniently located RFID reader. What NFC brings to Walsh's vision is that a dedicated RFID reader may no longer be necessary; a patron could use their own NFC- enabled smartphone to read a tag rather than taking it to a special location to be read. Indeed, with NFC, library records and metadata could theoretically be stored on and retrieved from library physical holdings themselves, allowing a patron tap a book or resource borrowed from the library to recall its title, author, and due date. An exciting and immediate use for NFC in libraries is for self- checkout: a patron can browse the stacks and could tap an NFC-tagged book with their NFC enabled phone to check it out without visiting the circulation desk or waiting in line.[154]

6.7. RECOMMENDATIONS

According to McHugh and Yarmey[145] the implementation of NFC has been slow and unsteady and they do not foresee an immediate implementation in libraries. However, they recommend that librarians learn and prepare for NFC. They recommend for example:

- Follow the progress of research and scholarship on NFC and commercial progress of NFC technology to better anticipate its adoption in your community.
- Experiment with NFC technology and develop prototype applications for NFC use in the library.
- Offering an informational workshop on NFC for users and library colleagues.
- Enquire from the RFID vendor about tag compatibility with NFC and rewriting the tags.
- Monitor the progress of security and privacy aspects of NFC technology and educate the users about these issues. Develop or update your library security policy.
- Allow patrons to "opt-in" to any NFC services at your library, providing other modes of communication where possible.
- Develop and share best practices for NFC implementations.
- Support research on NFC in libraries via planning grants, research forums, and conference sessions.

6.8. CONCLUSION

Beyond the potential benefits of NFC, librarians should also be aware of and prepared for privacy and security concerns that accompany the technology. User privacy is of the utmost concern. NFC involves users' mobile devices generating, collecting, storing, and sharing a significant amount of personal data. Several of these, particularly mobile payment necessitate the exchange of highly confidential data, including but not limited to a user's financial accounts, purchase history, etc. Spam may also be a concern; sending unwanted content (for example, advertisements, coupons, or adware) to users' mobile devices without their consent. Librarians should also use special caution when considering the implementation of NFC for library promotions or services. Security is a significant concern and an active area of research, as many NFC implementations involve the exchange of sensitive financial or otherwise personal data. An important concept in NFC security, particularly in the context of mobile payment, is the idea of a tamper- proof "secure element" (SE) as a basic protection for sensitive or confidential data such as account information and credentials for authentication.[155]

Outside of continued standardization, the most effective measures for protecting NFC data transmissions are data encryption and secondly the establishment of a secure channel between the sending and receiving devices (e.g., using a key agreement protocol and/or via SSL). For security concerns, as with privacy concerns, librarians have a crucial role to play in user education. There are important steps that individual users can and should take to protect their devices—for example, setting a lock code for their device, knowing how to remotely wipe a stolen phone, and installing and regularly updating antivirus software. However, many users are unaware of the vulnerability of their mobile devices and often fail to enact even basic protections.

Considering the potential implications of NFC technology, both positive and negative the following points must be considered by library professionals before the use of this technology: Privacy and Confidentiality Guidelines to reflect potential applications and risks of NFC must be kept in mind. They should support research on NFC in libraries via planning grants, research forums, and conference sessions. Fostering of professional discussion of NFC via incorporation into related interest groups is another way to develop a better understanding of the technology. They should develop and share best practices for NFC implementations.

By empowering objects and people to communicate with each other at a different level and establish a "touch to share" paradigm, NFC technology has the potential to transform the information environment surrounding our libraries and fundamentally alter the ways in which the library patrons interact with information.

References

1. Al-Ani, Muzhir, Shaban. (2015). Packages tracking using RFID technology. *International Journal of Business and ICT.* 1 (3-4), 12-20. Retrieved from http://docs.wixstatic.com/ugd/4f5010_fb1bd0ca590340929e8b3c495fa47cc3.pdf
2. Ahson S.,& Ilyas M. (2008). *RFID handbook: Applications, technology, security and privacy.* Florida: CRC press. Retrieved from http://ec-wu.at/spiekermann/publications/inbooks/ons%20security%20in%20rfid%20handbook.pdf
3. Ankur (n.d). *Security issues in RFID* (Unpublished doctoral dissertation). KTH Royal Institute of Technology, Sweeden. Retrieved from http://cwi.unik.no/images/Introduction_to_RFID.pdf
4. Embry, W. (n.d.). *Are you ready for RFID? The promise and challenges of implementing Radio Frequency Identification (RFID) systems across the extended supply chain SAS.* Retrieved from
5. *https://www.slideshare.net/PeterSam67/are-you-ready-for-rfid-the-promise-and-challenges-of*
6. Brown, D. (2007). *RFID implementation.* New York: McGraw-Hill.
7. Macmillan Dictionary and Thesaurus: Free English Dictionary Online. *RFID.* Retrieved from *http://www.macmillandictionary.com/diction*
8. Automatic Identification and Data Capture (AIDC). *RFID.* Retrieved from https://searcherp.techtarget.com/definition/Automatic-Identification-and-Data-Capture-AIDC
9. Marsterson, W., Ward, M., Birchall, A. J., Hopkinson, A., Van K. R. & Kelly, K. (2006). *RFID: Frequency, standards,*

adoption and innovation (JISC Technology and Standards Watch). London: Middlesex University Research Repository. Retrieved from *https://eprints.mdx.ac.uk/2990/*

10. Violino, Bob (2005). *The history of RFID technology.* Retrieved from *https://www.rfidjournal.com/articles/view?1338*

11. Liu, Haidi (2007). *Radio Frequency Identification (RFID) adoption in the South African retail sector: An investigation of perceptions held by members of the retail sector regarding the adoption constraints* (Unpublished master dissertation). Rhodes University, Grahamstown, South Africa. Retrieved from http://www.ejise.com/issue/download.html?idArticle=650

12. J. Landt, "The history of RFID," in IEEE Potentials, vol. 24, no. 4, pp. 8-11, Oct.-Nov. 2005. doi: 10.1109/MP.2005.1549751

13. Stockman, H. (1948).Communication by means of reflected power. *Proceedings of the Institute of Radio Engineers.* Retrieved from *http://simson.net/ref/ 1948/stockman.pdf*

14. Hunt, V. (2007). *RFID: A guide to radio frequency identification.* Hoboken, New Jersey: Wiley- Interscicnce. Retrieved from *http:// onlinelibrary.wiley.com/doi/10.1002/97804 70112250.fmatter/pdf*

15. SATO DCS and Labelling worldwide.(2004). *The RFID guidebook* (Rev.8). Retrieved from *http://www.satoeurope.com/sites/europe/Uploads/Files/Products/Sato%20RFID/RFID%20Guide.pdf*

16. Violino, Bob (2005). *The history of RFID technology.* Retrieved from *https://www.rfidjournal.com/articles/view?1338&_ga=2.42462883.740452482.1541251181-1562861806.1541251181*

17. Hunt, V. D., Puglia, A., & Puglia, M. (2006). *RFID- A Guide to Radio Frequency Identification.* Hoboken, New Jersey: Wiley Interscience. Retrieved from *http://onlinelibrary.wiley.com/doi/10.100 2/ 9780470112250.fmatter/pdf*

18. Steve, Hodges, & Duncan, McFarlane (2005). *Radio Frequency Identification: Technology, applications and impact.* Retrieved from https://pdfs.semanticscholar.org/0905/d36ef9a12cd34145891 85c3f33ac7de6fd8e.pdf

19. Landt, Jeremy (2001). *Shrouds of time the history of RFID.* Pittsburgh, PA: Association for Automatic Identification and

Data Capture Technology. Retrieved from https://www.transcore.com/wp-content/uploads/2017/01/History-of-RFID-White-Paper.pdf

20. Frequently Asked Questions.*RFID Journal*. Retrieved from *http://www.rfidjournal.com/faq/*

21. Lewis, S. (2004). *A basic introduction to RFID technology and its use in the supply chain*. Retrieved from https://mthink.com/legacy/www.ascet.com/content/pdf/ASC6_wp_lewis.pdf

22. JESIC Technology Limited. (2008). *Radio Frequency Identification (RFID)*.Retrived from *http://www.jesic-tech.com/RFID.html*

23. Ahson, S., & Ilyas, M. (2008).*RFID handbook: Applications, technology, security and privacy*. Boca Raton: CRC Press.

24. Holloway, Simon (2006). *RFID: An introduction*. Retrieved from https://studylib.net/doc/7469981/rfid—an-introduction—center

25. Hitachi Limited. (2006). *World's smallest and thinnest 0.15 x 0.15 mm, 7.5µm thick RFID IC chip*. Retrieved from https://www.hitachi.com/New/cnews/060206.pdf

26. Ward, M., Kranenburg, R.V., & Backhouse, G. (2006). *RFID: Frequency, standards, adoption and innovation* (JISC Technology and Standard Watch). Retrieved from http://citeseerx.ist.psu.edu/viewdoc/download?doi= 10.1.1.102.3390&rep=rep1&type=pdf

27. Repanovivi, A.,& Cristea, L. (2011). *RFID- Application in info-documentary systems*. In Designing and deplyoing RFID applications. Retrieved from *http://cdn.intechweb.org/pdfs/18102.pdf*

28. Accenture (2011).*Radio Frequency Identification (RFID)*. Retrieved from *http:// www. thetawer .com/ wp-content/uploads/2011/10/a.-Whitepaper- Radiofrequency-Identification.pdf.*

29. Bhuptani, M., & Moradpour, S. (2005). *RFID Field Guide: Deploying Radio Frequency Identification systems*. New Jersey: Prentice Hall. Retrieved from *http://my.Safaribook son line.com/book/ hardware/rfid/0131853554*

30. Boss, Richard, W.(2011). *RFID technology for libraries*. Retrieved from *http://www.ala.org /pla/ tools/%20technotes/rfidtechnology*

31. Finkenzeller, K. (2012). *RFID Handbook: Fundamentals and Applications in Contactless Smart Cards and Identiûcation.* Retrived from *http://aries.ektf.hu/~dream/e107/e107_files/downloads/rfidhand.pdf*

32. Accenture (2011). *Radio Frequency Identification (RFID).* Retrieved from *http://www. thetawer .com/ wp-content/uploads/2011/10/a.-Whitepaper- Radiofrequency-Identification.pdf.*

33. RFID Frequencies. Retrieved from http://www.docin.com/p-189022887.html

34. NISO (2012). *RFID in U.S. libraries.* Retrieved from https://groups.niso.org/apps/group_public/download.php/8269/RP-6-2012_RFID-in_US_Libraries.pdf

35. Lewis, S. (2004). *A basic introduction to RFID technology and its use in the supply chain.* Retrieved from https://mthink.com/legacy/www.ascet.com/content/pdf/ASC6_wp_lewis.pdf

36. Violino, Bob. A Summary of RFID Standards retrieved from https://www.rfidjournal.com/articles/view?1335/3

37. Tutorial Rcports.com (2013). *RFID standards.* Retrieved from http://www.tutorial-reports.com/wireless/rfid/standards.php

38. GS1 India. (2014). *EPCglobal standards.* Retrieved from https://www.gs1.org/standards/epc-rfid

39. Clampitt, H. (2004). *The RFID handbook.* Retrieved from *http://rfidhandbook.blogspot.com/*

40. Reitz, Joan M (2004). *Dictionary for library and Information science.* London: Libraries Unlimited. Retrieved from https://repository.wcsu.edu/library_books/1/

41. Prytherch, R. (2005). *Harrod's librarians' glossary and reference book : A directory of over 10,200 terms, organizations, projects and acronyms in the areas of information management, library science, publishing and archive management.* Aldershot, Hants, England Burlington, VT: Ashgate.

42. Chachra, V. (2003). *Experiences in implementing VTLS RFID solutions in a multi-vendor environment.* World Library and Information Congress: 69th IFLA General Conference and Council 1-9 August 2003. Retrieved from https://archive.ifla.org/IV/ifla69/papers/132e-Chachra.pdf

43. Yu, S.C. (2008). Implementation of an innovative RFID application in libraries. *Library Hi Tech*, 26(3), 398-410. doi: 10.1108/07378830810903328

44. Singh, J., Brar, N., & Fong, C. (2006). The state of RFID applications in libraries.*Information Technology and Libraries*, 25(1), 24-32. doi: 10.6017/ital.v25i1.3326

45. Pandey, P., & Mahajan, K.D. (2012). *Application of RFID technology in libraries and role of librarian.* Paper presented in the 12th MANLIBNET Convention 2010, Jaipur. Retrieved from *http:// eprints.rclis.org/ 15253/ 3/ RFID.pdf*

46. Ghosh, T. B. (2007). *Application of RFID technology in SardarVallabhbhai National Institute of Technology (SVNIT), Surat.* Paper presented at the National Workshop on ICT Application in Library Automation-2007, Allahabad (India). Retrieved from *http://eprints.rclis.org/ 11357/ 1/ RFID_paper_*Alahabad%5B1%5D.pdf

47. LibBest (2014). *Library RFID system - Shelf management.* Retrieved from *http://www.rfid- library.com/ shelf.html*

48. Shahid, Syed M. (2005). Use of RFID technology in libraries: A new approach to circulation, tracking, inventorying and security of library materials. *Library Philosophy and Practice*, 8(1). Retrieved from *http://unllib.unl.edu/LPP/shahid.htm*

49. Needleman, M., Bodfish, J., O'Brien, T., Rush, J.E., & Stevens, P. (2001). The NISO circulation interchange protocol (NCIP) – an XML based standard. *Library Hi Tech*, 19(3), 223–230. doi: 10.1108/07378830110405526

50. LibBest (2014).*System architecture.* Retrieved from http://www.rfid-library.com/

51. Molnar, D., & Wagner, D. (2004). *Privacy and security in library RFID: Issues, practices and architectures.* Proceeding CCS '04 Proceedings of the 11th ACM conference on Computer and communications security ACM New York, 210- 219.Retrieved from *https://dl.acm.org/citation.cfm?id=1030112*

52. Vasishta, Seema (2009). *Roadmap for RFID implementation in Central library, PEC University of Technology.* Paper presented in the International Conference on Academic Libraries, Delhi. Retrieved from http://eprints.rclis.org/17693/

53. Ayre, Lori B. (2006). RFID and libraries. In George M Eberhart (Ed.).*The whole library handbook: Current data professional*

advice and curiosa about libraries and library services (pp.452-454). Chicago: American Library Association.

54. Narayanan A., Singh, Sanjay & Somasekharan M.(2005) *Implementing RFID in library: Methodologies, advantages and disadvantages.* Paper presented at the Conference on Recent Advances in Information Technology, IGCAR – Kalpakkam, July 14-15, Kalpakkam. Retrieved http://www.libsys.co.in/download/implementing_rfid_in_Libraries.pdf

55. Boss, Richard W. (2004).*RFID technology for libraries.* American Library Association. Retrieved from https://alair.ala.org/bitstream/handle/11213/258/RFID.pdf?sequence=108&isAllowed=y

56. Chia, Christopher (2001). Transformation of libraries in Singapore. *Library review*, 50(7/8), 343- 348.doi: 0.1108/EUM0000000006071

57. Yorkovich, John D. (2001). Lied Library: at the forefront of technology with 3M digital ID collection management. *New Library World*, 102(6), 216–221. doi: 10.1108 /03074800 11039 4596

58. Yuan, Kho, Hao, Hong, Ang Chip, Ang, M., &Peng, GoiSio. (2002). *Unmanned librury: an intelligent robotic books retrieval & return system utilizing RFID tags.* Paper Presented on the IEEE International Conference on system, Man and Cybernetics: Bridging the Digital Divide for Cyber-development, Human Progress, Understanding and Prosperity, Hammamet – Tunisia. doi:10.1109/ICSMC.2002.1173317

59. Fabbi, Jennifer L., Watson, Sidney D., & Marks, Kenneth E. (2002). Implementation of the 3M™ Digital Identification System at the UNLV libraries. *Library Hi Tech*, 20(1), 104–110. doi: 10.1108/ 07378830210420726

60. Ngian, LekChoh (2003). A Totally Do-It-Yourself Library without a Library Customer Service Desk: The Singapore Experience. *IFLA Journal*, 29, 298- 300. doi: 10.1177/ 03400 3520302900405

61. Kern, Christian (2004).Radio-Frequency- Identification for security and media circulation in libraries.*Electronic Library*, 22 (4), 317 – 324. doi: 10.1108/02640470410552947

62. Kern, C.,& Nauer, M. (2004). Implementing RFID in libraries for process automation experiences from over twenty current installations. *LIBER Quarterly*, 14(2). Retrieved from https:/

/www.liberquarterly.eu/articles/10.18352/lq.7772/

63. Sheck, Marilyn (2004). Meeting new challenges with new technology: The Seattle Public Library experience. *Library Hi Tech News*, 21(10), 22–27. doi: 10.1108/07419050410577578

64. Molnar, D., & Wagner, D. (2004). *Privacy and security in Library RFID: Issues, practices and architectures.* Proceeding CCS '04 Proceedings of the 11th ACM conference on Computer and communications security ACM New York, 210-219. Retrieved from https://dl.acm.org/citation.cfm?id=1030112

65. Rafiq, Muhammad (2005). *Radio Frequency Identification (RFID): Its usage and libraries.* Retrieved from https://core.ac.uk/download/pdf/11878395.pdf

66. Fabbi, Jennifer L., Watson, Sidney D., Marks, Kenneth E., & Sylvis, Zep (2005). UNLV Libraries and the digital identification frontier. *Library Hi Tech*, 23(3), 313–322. doi: 10.1108/ 07378830510621739

67. Karen, Coyle (2005). Management of RFID in libraries. *The Journal of Academic Librarianship*, 31(5), 486–489. doi: 10.1016/j.acalib.2005.06.001

68. Dawes, Trevor A. (2005). Is RFID right for your library?. *Journal of Access Services*, 2(4), 7-13. doi: 10.1300/J204v02n04_02

69. Hopkinson, A., & Chandrakar, R. (2006). Introducing RFID at Middlesex University Learning Resources. *Program: Electronic Library and Information systems*, 40(1), 89-97. doi: 10.1108/ 00330330610646834

70. Palmer, Martin (2006). Using RFID to transform Essex Libraries. *Library Hi Tech News*, 23(10), 21– 22. doi: 10.1108/07419050610730070

71. Singh, J., Brar, N., & Fong, C. (2006). The state of RFID applications in libraries. *Information Technology and Libraries*, 25(1), 24-32. doi: 10.6017/ital.v25i1.3326

72. Shamsudin, T.M.W., Salami, Momoh J.E., & Martono, W. (2007). *RFID-based intelligent books shelving system.* Paper presented at the IEEE 1st Annual RFID Eurasia, Istanbul. doi: 10.1109/ RFIDEURASIA.2007.4368105

73. Curtin, J., Kauffman, Robert J., & Riggins, Frederick J. (2007). Making the 'most' out of RFID technology: A research

agenda for the study of the adoption, usage and impact of RFID. *Information Technology and Management*, 8(2), 87-110. doi: 10.1007/s10799-007-0010-1

74. Shien-Chiang, Yu (2007). RFID implementation and benefits in libraries. *The Electronic Library*, 25(1), 54-64. doi: 10.1108/02640470710729119

75. Kevin, C., & Martin, P. (2007). A primer on Radio Frequency Identification for libraries. *Library Hi Tech*, 25(4), 595–611. doi: 10.1108/ 07378830710840536

76. Potdar, V., Hayati, P., & Chang, E. (2007). *Improving RFID read rate reliability by a systematic error detection approach.* Paper presented at the IEEE 1st Annual RFID Eurasia, Istanbul. doi: 10.1109/ RFIDEURASIA.2007.4368118

77. Gómez-Gómez, A., Ena-Rodríguez, B., & Priore, P. (2007). RFID in library management and maintenance. *El Professional De La Information*, 16(4), 319-328.Retrieved from http://www.elprofesionaldelainformacion.com/contenidos/2007/julio/05.pdf

78. So, Stuart C.K., & Liu, John J. (2007). Learning from failure: A case study of adopting Radio Frequency Identification technology in library services. *International Journal of Technology Intelligence and Planning,* 3(1), 75-95. Retrieved from *https://trove.nla.gov.au/work/162349519?q&versionId=176941516*

79. Muir, Scott P. (2007). RFID security concerns. *Library Hi Tech*, 25(1), 95-107. doi: 10.1108/ 07378830710735885

80. Butters, Alan (2007). RFID systems, standards and privacy within libraries. *The Electronic Library*, 25(4), 430-439. doi: 10.1108/02640470710779844

81. Butters, A. (2008). RFID in Australian academic libraries: Exploring the barriers to implementation. *Australian Academic and Research Libraries*, 39(3), 198-206. Retrieved from https://www.tandfonline.com/doi/abs/10.1080/00048623.2008.10721350

82. Butters, A. (2008). RFID for libraries: A comparison of high frequency and ultra high frequency options. *APLIS*,21(3), 120-134. Retrieved from *http://web.b.ebscohost.com/abstract?site=ehost&scope=site&jrnl=10305033&asa=Y&AN=34141275&h=b1tAR7nO9NGitHN%2bkjYHtcVuORUUgeQrV3IZ8unGRyNfvgQ3mZfi43QoIKHrP7NiSJA%2foJmet6NpSDwBxkDzhQ%3d%3d&crl=c*

&resultLocal=ErrCrlNoResults&resultNs=Ehost&crlhashurl=login.aspx%3fdirect%3dtrue%26profile%3dehost%26scope%3dsite%26authtype%3dcrawler%26jrnl%3d10305033%26asa%3dY%26AN%3d34141275

83. Yu, S.C. (2008). Implementation of an innovative RFID application in libraries. *Library Hi Tech*, 26(3), 398-410. doi: 10.1108/07378830810903328

84. Golding, P., & Tennant, V. (2007). Performance testing: evaluating an RFID library inventory reader. *International Journal of Internet Protocol Technology (IJIPT)*, 2(3/4), 240-251. Doi: 10.1504/IJIPT.2007.016224

85. Golding, P., & Tennant, V. (2008). Evaluation of a Radio Frequency Identification (RFID) library system: Preliminary results. *International Journal of Multimedia and Ubiquitous Engineering*, 3(1), 118. Retrieved from https://www.researchgate.net/publication/228894339_Evaluation_of_a_Radio_Frequency_Identification _RFID_Library_System_Preliminary_Results

86. Lau, P.-Y., Yung, K. K-O., & Yung, E. K.-N.(2008). *A smart bookshelf for library RFID system.* Paper presented at the IEEE Proceedings of Asia Pacific Microwave Conference, Macau. doi: 10.1109/ APMC.2008.4958058

87. Ching, Steve, H., & Tai, Alice (2009). HF RFID versus UHF RFID — Technology for library service transformation at City University of Hong Kong. *The Journal of Academic Librarianship*, 35(4), 347-359. doi: http://dx.doi.org/10.1016/j.acalib.2009. 04.005

88. Robkin, S. (2009). Managing multivendor RFID rollouts. *American Libraries*, 40(11), 44-47. Retrieved from *http://connection.ebscohost.com/c/ articles/45315236/managing-multivendor-rfid- rollouts*

89. Bahri, Shamshul (2010). *Enhancing the delivery of library's services through the implementation of an emerging information technology: A process framework*. Paper presented at the PACIFIC Asia Conference on Information Systems, Taipei, Taiwan, 9-12 July 2010. Retrieved form *https://aisel.aisnet.org/pacis2010/189/*

90. Blansit, Douglas B. (2010). RFID terminology and technology: Preparing to evaluate RFID for your library. *Journal of Electronic Resources in Medical Libraries*, 7(4), 344-354. Retrieved from *https://www.tandfonline.com/doi/abs/*

10.1080/15424065.2010.527255

91. Caldwell-Stone, Deborah (2010). RFID in libraries. *Library Technology Reports*, 46(8), 38 44. doi:10.5860/ltr.46n8

92. Cunningham, Matthew S. (2010). *A case study into the implementation of RFID at the Pilkington Library Loughborough University.* (Unpublished Master's dissertation). Retrieved from *https://dspace.lboro.ac.uk/dspace-jspui/handle/2134/8820*

93. Feng, Cheng (2010). *Research for application of RFID in library.* Paper presented at the IEEE International Conference on Computer and Communication Technologies in Agriculture Engineering, Chengdu. doi: 10.1109/CCTAE.2010.5544208

94. Ustundag, A., & Kilinc, M.S. (2010). *Design and development of RFID based library information system.* Paper presented at the proceedings of the 14th World Multi-Conference on Systemics, Cybernetics and Informatics, Florida, USA. Retrieved from https://pdfs.semanticscholar.org/a891/6df2e8c39e5e85ab488a8e920c8f98f7a917.pdf

95. Zhu, C-P., Wang, Z., Deng, J-X., Gu, H., Shan, M- L., Han, Q-B., & Zhang, S. (2010). *Design of an intelligent book conveyor based on RFID.* Paper presented at the IEEE 2nd International Conference on Information Science and Engineering, Hangzhou, China. doi: 10.1109/ICISE.2010.5691717

96. Abdullah, A.T.B., Ismail, I.B., Ibrahim, A.B., & Noor, M.Z.H.B. (2011). *Library shelf management system using RFID technology.* Paper presented at the IEEE International Conference on System Engineering and Technology, ICSET 2011, 215-218. doi: 10.1109/ICSEngT.2011.5993453

97. Mehrjerdi, Yahia Z. (2011).RFID: The big player in the libraries of the future. *The Electronic Library*, 29(1), 36–51. doi: 10.1108/02640471111111424

98. Repanovici, A., & Cristea, L. (2011). RFID technology used in small library - case study at transilvania university. *Romanian Review Precision Mechanics, Optics and Mechatronics*, 39, 109-112. Retrieved from *https://www.researchgate.net/publication/292827064_RFID_technology_used_in_small_library_-_case_study_at_transilvania_university*

99. Walsh, Andrew (2011). Blurring the boundaries between our

physical and electronic libraries: Location-aware technologies, QR codes and RFID tags. *The Electronic Library*, 29(4), 429–437.Retrieved form *http://www.emeraldinsight.com/ journals.htm?issn=02640473&volume=29&issue=4&articleid=1944329&show=html*

100. Zimerman, Martin (2011). Radio Frequency Identification (RFID): Time to take another look. *OCLC Systems & Services*, 27(2), 146–154. Doi: https://doi.org/10.1108/10650751111135436

101. Gibb, F., Thornley, C.V., Ferguson, S., & Weckert, J. (2011). The application of RFIDs in libraries: An assessment of technological, management and professional issues. *International Journal of Information Management*, 31(3), 244-251. Retrieved form *http:// researchrepository .ucd.ie/ bitstream /handle/10197/3587/IJIM-D-10-00073.pdf?sequence=1*

102. Thornley, C., Ferguson, S., Weckert, J., & Gibb, F. (2011). Do RFIDs (Radio Frequency Identifier Devices) provide new ethical dilemmas for librarians and information professionals?.*International of Information Management*, 31(6), 546–555. doi: 10.1016/j.ijinfomgt.2011.02.006

103. Ayre, Lori B. (2012). Library RFID systems for identification, security, and materials handling. *Library Technology Reports*, 48(5),9-16. doi: 10.5860/ltr.48n5

104. Sun, H-C., & Chen, K-N. (2012). A proposed model for library stacks management. *Library Collections, Acquisitions, and Technical Services*, 36(1–2), 24–29. doi: http://dx.doi.org/10.1016/j.lcats.2012. 04.001

105. Dwivedi, Y.K., Kapoor, K.K., Williams, M.D., & Williams, J. (2013). RFID systems in libraries: An empirical examination of factors affecting system use and user satisfaction. *International Journal ofInformation Management*, 33(2) 367–377. doi: *http://dx.doi.* org/10.1016/j.ijinfomgt.2012.10.008

106. Makori, E. (2013). Adoption of Radio Frequency Identification technology in university libraries: A Kenyan perspective. *The Electronic Library*, 31(2), 208-216.doi:10.1108/02640471311312384

107. Sugie, N. (2013). Application of Radio Frequency Identification technology to study library users' information-seeking behavior. *Library & Information Science Research*,

35(1), 69–77. doi: http://dx.doi.org/10.1016/j.lisr.2012.06.0 06

108. Zhang, M. (2013). Study on intelligent library system based on RFID technology. *International Journal of Digital Content Technology and its Applications*, 7(5), 16-24. Retrieved from *http://www.globalcis.org/jdcta/ppl/JDCTA2695PPL.pdf*

109. Guo, Jing, Huang, Qinling & Chen, Jiayi (2014) "A study of UHF-RFID data model construction in university libraries", *The Electronic Library*, 32 (5), 726-741, https://doi.org/10.1108/EL-10-2013-0177

110. Fujisaki, K. (2015). An RFID-based System for Library Management and Its Performance Evaluation. In Ninth International Conference on Complex, Intelligent, and Software Intensive Systems, Blumenau, 2015, 105-109. doi: 10.1109/CISIS.2015.15

111. Timoshenko, I. V. (2016). The application of the radio frequency identification technology at libraries: The Russian experience. Scientific and Technical Information Processing, 43(3), 189-193. doi:10.3103/s0147688216030126

112. Sammeta, S. G. & Madara, S. R. (2018). Recent trends in RFID technologies and its impact on universities. In Advances in Science and Engineering Technology International Conferences (ASET), Abu Dhabi, 2018, 1-6. doi: 10.1109/ICASET.2018.8376922

113. Shahid, Syed M. (2005). Use of RFID technology in libraries: A new approach to circulation, tracking, inventorying, and security of library materials. *Library Philosophy and Practice*, 8(1). Retrieved from http://unllib.unl.edu/LPP/shahid.htm

114. Narayanan A., Sanjay Singh, & Somasekharan M. (2005). *Implementing RFID in library: Methodologies, advantages and disadvantages*. Paper presented at the Conference on Recent Advances in Information Technology, IGCAR – Kalpakkam, July 14-15, Kalpakkam. Retrieved from http://www.libsys.co.in/download/implementing_rfid_in_Libraries.pdf

115. NagaLakshmi, V., Rameshbabu, I., & Lalitha, Bhaskari D. (2006). A security mechanism for library management system using low cost RFID tags. *Journal of Systemics, Cybernetics and Informatics*, 5 (1), 92-96. Retrieved from *http://citeseerx.ist.psu.edu/viewdoc/download?doi=10.1.1.566.8813&rep=rep1&type=pdf*

116. Selamat, M.S., & Majlis, B.Y. (2006). *Challenges in implementing RFID tag in a conventional library.* Paper presented at the IEEE International Conference on Semiconductor Electronics, Kuala Lumpur. doi: 10.1109/ SMELEC.2006.381060

117. Kumar, Manoj, Murjani, Geeta G., & Patel, Bansari M. (2007). *Development of RFID interface for LMS: Solutions and techniques.* Paper presented at the Computer Science and IT Education Conference, Mauritius. Retrieved from https:/ /www.researchgate.net/publication/228419096_ Development_ of_RFID_Interface_for_LMS_Solutions _and_Techniques

118. Ghosh, T. B. (2007). *Application of RFID technology in SardarVallabhbhai National Institute of Technology (SVNIT), Surat.* Paper presented at the National Workshop on ICT Application in Library Automation-2007, Allahabad (India). Retrieved from http://eprints.rclis.org/11357/

119. Pattanaik, Bibhuti B., & Pattnaik, B. (2007). *RFID: The security for library.* Paper presented at the 10th National Convention on Knowledge, Library and Information Networking, Libraries without boundaries: Reaching the Unreachable in Knowledge Era, New Delhi (India). Retrieved from *RFID: The security for library.* Paper presented at the 10th National Convention on Knowledge, Library and Information Networking, Libraries without

120. Singh, G., & Midha, M. (2008). RFID: A new technology in library management systems. *Journal of Interlibrary Loan, Document Delivery and Electronic Reserve*, 18(4), 439-447. Retrieved from *http://www.tandfonline.com/doi/pdf/ 10.1080/ 10723030 802181778*

121. Galhotra, M.K., & Galhotra A.M. (2009). Application of Radio Frequency Identification Technology in libraries. *DESIDOC Journal of Library and Information Technology*, 29(3), 59-64.

122. Bansode, Sadanand Y., & Desale, Sanjay K. (2009). Implementation of RFID technology in University of Pune Library.*Program: Electronic Library and Information Systems*, 43(2), 202–214. doi: 10.1108/ 00330330910954406

123. Vasishta, Seema (2009). *Roadmap for RFID implementation in Central Library, PEC University of Technology.* Paper presented in the International Conference on Academic Libraries, Delhi. Retrieved from http://eprints.rclis.org/ 17693/

124. Margam, Madhusudhan (2010). RFID technology implementation in two libraries in New Delhi. *Program: Electronic Library and Information Systems*, 44(2), 149–157. doi: 10.1108/ 00330331011039508

125. Radha, L. (2011). Deployment of RFID (Radio Frequency Identification) at Indian academic libraries: Issues and best practice. *International Journal of Library and Information Science*, 3(2), 34-37.Retrieved from http://www.academicjournals.org/app/webroot/article/article1379512040_Radha.pdf

126. Pandey, P., & Mahajan, K.D. (2012). *Application of RFID technology in libraries and role of librarian.* Paper presented in the 12th MANLIBNET Convention 2010, Jaipur. Retrieved from *http:// eprints.rclis.org/ 15253/3/RFID.pdf*

127. Prasanna, K. and Megalan Leo, L.. (2015). Library automation system using RFID: Survey. International Journal of Applied Engineering Research, 10(20), 15705-15709

128. Singh, Neeraj Kumar & Mahajan, Preeti, (2017). "Application of Radio Frequency Identification Technology in libraries and information centres: An Indian perspective". *Library Philosophy and Practice* (e-journal). 1614. http://digitalcommons.unl.edu/libphilprac/1614

129. Engel, Elena (2006). *RFID Implementations in California Libraries: Costs and Benefits.* Retrieved from https://www.kcoyle.net/RFIDCostsBenefits.pdf

130. Ali, D. A. (2015). Near-Field Communication Technology and Its Impact in Smart University and Digital Library: Comprehensive Study. *Journal of Library and Information Sciences*, 3(2). doi:10.15640/jlis.v3n2a4

131. Unitag. (n.d.). *NFC technology Discover what NFC is, and how to use it.* Retrieved from https://www.unitag.io/nfc/what-is-nfc

132. Kalapala, A. (2013, July). *Analysis of Near Field Communication (NFC) and other Short ...* Retrieved from http://www.idrbt.ac.in/assets/alumni/PT-2013/Apuroop%20Kalapala_ Analysis%20of%20Near%20Field%20Communication% 20(NFC)%20and%20other%20short%20range %20mobile%20communication%20technologies_2013.pdf

133. *NFC Technology.* (n.d.). Retrieved from https://

www.radioelectronics.com/info/wireless/nfc/nfc-near-field-communications-technology.php

134. *Near field communication vs Radio frequency identification.* Retrieved from http://www.nfcnearfieldcommunication.org/radio-frequency.html

135. Andrew (2011). *Difference Between RFID and NFC.* Retrieved from https://www.differencebetween.com/difference-between-rfid-and-vs-nfc/

136. NFC Forum. (n.d.). *What It Does.* Retrieved from https://nfc-forum.org/what-is-nfc/what-it-does

137. Android Authority (2018.). *How NFC works?* Retrieved from https://www.androidauthority.com/what-is-nfc-270730/

138. Coskun, V., Ozdenizci, B., & Ok, K. (2015). The Survey on Near Field Communication. *Sensors,* 15(6), 13348-13405. doi:10.3390/s150613348

139. Ruth, C. (2009). NFC Forum Calls for Breakthrough Solutions for Annual Competition. Retrieved from https://nfc-forum.org/newsroom/nfc-forum-calls-for-breakthrough-solutions-for-annual-competition/

140. Roland, M. (2011). *Near Field Communication (NFC) Technology and Measurements* ... Retrieved from https://cdn.rohde-schwarz.com/pws/dl_downloads/dl_application/application_notes/1ma182/1MA182_5E_NFC_WHITE_PAPER.pdf

141. Profis, S. (2014, September 05). *Everything you need to know about NFC and mobile payments.* Retrieved from https://www.cnet.com/how-to/how-nfc-works-and-mobile-payments/

142. *The 5 NFC Tag Types.* (n.d.). Retrieved from https://www.dummies.com/consumer-electronics/5-nfc-tag-types/

143. Ramos-De-Luna, I., Montoro-Ríos, F., Liébana-Cabanillas, F., & Luna, J. G. (2017). NFC technology acceptance for mobile payments: A Brazilian Perspective. *Review of Business Management,* 19(63), 82-103. doi:10.7819/rbgn.v0i0.2315

144. Du, H. (2013). NFC Technology: Today and Tomorrow. *International Journal of Future Computer and Communication,* 351-354. doi:10.7763/ijfcc.2013.v2.183

145. McHugh, S., & Yarmey, K. (2014). *Near field communication: Recent developments and library implications. Synthesis Lectures on Emerging Trends in Librarianship. 1 (1), 1-93.*

Retrieved from https://www.morganclaypool.com/doi/pdf/10.2200/S00570ED1V01Y201403ETL002

146. Sukeshinirt, T. S. (2013). NFC Technology and Social Networking. *International Journal Of Engineering And Computer Science*, 2(11), 3114-3116. Retrieved from https://www.ijecs.in/index.php/ijecs/article/view/2132

147. Boyle, T. (2013, July 01). *NFC and Social Media.* Retrieved from https://qfuse.com/blog/nfc-and-social-media/

148. SmartTech. (n.d.). *Gaming applications with RFID and NFC technology.* Retrieved from https://www.smart-tec.com/en/applications/gaming

149. Yusof, M. K., Abel, A., Saman, M. Y., & Rahman, M. N. (2015). Adoption of near field communication in S-Library application for information science. *New Library World*, 116(11/12), 728-747. doi:10.1108/nlw-02-2015-0014

150. Ali, D. A. (2015). Near-Field Communication Technology and Its Impact in Smart University and Digital Library: Comprehensive Study. *Journal of Library and Information Sciences*, 3(2), 43-78. doi:10.15640/jlis.v3n2a4

151. Rajiv. (2018, June 22). *Applications and Future of Near Field Communication.* Retrieved from https://www.rfpage.com/applications-near-field-communication-future/

152. Mchugh, S., & Yarmey, K. (2012). Near Field Communication: Introduction and Implications. *Journal of Web Librarianship*, 6(3), 186-207. doi:10.1080/19322909.2012.700610

153. Walsh, A. (2011). Blurring the boundaries between our physical and electronic libraries: Location-aware technologies, QR codes and RFID tags. *The Electronic Library*, 29(4), 429–437. DOI: 10.1108/02640471111156713. 3, 36

154. Roy, P. & Kumar, S. (2016). Application of RFID in Shaheed Rajguru College of Applied Sciences for Women Library, University of Delhi, India: Challenges and Future Prospects. *Qualitative and Quantitative Methods in Libraries, 5, pp- 117-130*

155. Jain, G., & Dahiya, S. (2015). NFC: Advantages, Limits and Future Scope. *International Journal on Cybernetics & Informatics*, 4(4), 1-12. doi:10.5121/ijci.2015.4401